T0288378

THE ARCHAEOLOGY OF ROMAN YORK

Adam Parker

AMBERLEY

First published 2019

Amberley Publishing
The Hill, Stroud
Gloucestershire, GL5 4EP

www.amberley-books.com

British Library Cataloguing in Publication Data.
A catalogue record for this book is available from the British Library.

ISBN 978 1 4456 8607 3 (print)
ISBN 978 1 4456 8608 0 (ebook)

Typesetting by Aura Technology and Software Services, India.
Printed in Great Britain.

Contents

Foreword

Roman archaeology is my passion, and after many years of working hands-on with York's incredible archaeological remains as part of the curatorial team of the Yorkshire Museum, it is both my pleasure and privilege to have written on this topic. The idea of writing this book was born out of a series of adult education courses run by the author at the University of York Centre for Lifelong Learning between 2013 and 2016. *Eboracum: Daily Life in Roman York*, *Magic and Religion in Roman Britain* and *Hadrian's Wall: A Frontier and Its People* were all enjoyable teaching experiences for me, but it was the passion and excitement of my adult students which have inspired this book and highlighted this gap in the current resources for the interested non-academic to learn about Roman York.

As this text is informed out of my own experience, there are many references made throughout to the archaeological collections in the Yorkshire Museum. I wish to take the time to thank both the hard-working staff of York Museums Trust and the interested and interesting visitors to this site for all the discussions and questions on Roman topics over the past few years, with special mention to my fellow archaeologists and historians Andrew Woods, Rebecca Griffiths, Emily Tilley and Natalie Buy variously for their support, discussions and encouragement. Thanks are also due to Patrick Ottaway for the image of the Altar of Marcus Aurelius Lunaris and for this excellent scholarship on the subject, and to Giles Darkes and Peter Addyman for arranging my use of the *Historic Towns Atlas* map of Roman York. I am always indebted to the fabulous Katherine Hughes for enduring the, inevitably, terrible weather on endless field trips to obscure Roman sites in Britain.

While the Yorkshire Museum is the best place in York to see the Roman archaeology first-hand and has the largest collection available for the public, for a holistic overview I also recommend visiting the undercroft of York Minster, the Roman Bath museum beneath the pub, and the city walls. As is the nature of York's incredible remains, it is worth bearing in mind that there is far more Roman archaeology hidden from view in the warehouses of museums and archaeological contractors, so there is always more to see.

I hope that this book proves to be interesting and that it can be used as a useful reference to the incredible archaeological remains of *Eboracum*.

AP
Autumn 2018

Introduction

York remains, to this day, a city of heritage. It is a place in which past and present collide and interweave. The standing heritage of York is, arguably, unparalleled in the north of England and the interest in York's past has shown that the same is true of what lies beneath the modern city. This situation has arisen because of the unbroken occupation of York since the arrival of the first Romans on the site in the second half of the first century AD. The modern city is a mix of twentieth-century, Victorian and Georgian building, built on top of and among the sprawling late medieval city, with its substantial precursors in the Norman, Anglo-Scandinavian, Anglian and Roman cities that existed here before it. Each period has left its own archaeological mark on the city, but none more so than the Roman period. Without the construction of the first timber fortress here by the soldiers of the 9th Legion, there would be no York as we understand it today.

York – a city of heritage. Looking north from the city walls, across the river and towards the Minster. (©Mattbuck via Wikimedia Commons [CC BY Attribution SA 2.0])

The position and layout of the modern city are still influenced by that of *Eboracum*. (©Peter Czerwinski via Wikimedia Commons [CC BY Attribution SA 4.0])

This book is designed for those with an interest in history and heritage, seeking an accessible introduction to the archaeology of York during the Roman period (AD 43–410). It is not a step-by-step tourist guide to the surviving remains, nor is it a formal academic treatise, but a handy synopsis of many aspects of the amazing evidence relating to a city famous for its Roman remains. In the coming chapters it will take a thematic approach to this subject, offering insight into the archaeological remains through topics and concepts rather than focussing on the chronological changes that happened from century to century.

The archaeological understanding of Roman York is based on centuries of investigation. This process of historical rediscovery really started in the Enlightenment period of the seventeenth and eighteenth centuries. Of course, the remains of Roman *Eboracum* have been known about for centuries – for example, the inscribed coffin of Marcus Verecundus, although eventually lost in the nineteenth century, was discovered in 1579. An altar to Jupiter was discovered in 1638 at Bishophill and the tombstone of Lucius Duccius Rufinus (a name which will be mentioned several times in this book) came to light in 1688.

The fortunes of York's archaeological discoveries were (and still are) tied to a need for large-scale building projects. The economic boom and expansion of York in the nineteenth and early twentieth centuries was the time when the vast majority of York's most famous Roman archaeological remains were discovered. Unhelpfully, this is the cause of a great number of problems for modern archaeologists. In some cases, the lack of useful information about where finds came from, the use of photographs, or even what happened to the objects themselves afterwards has hampered our full understanding of Roman York.

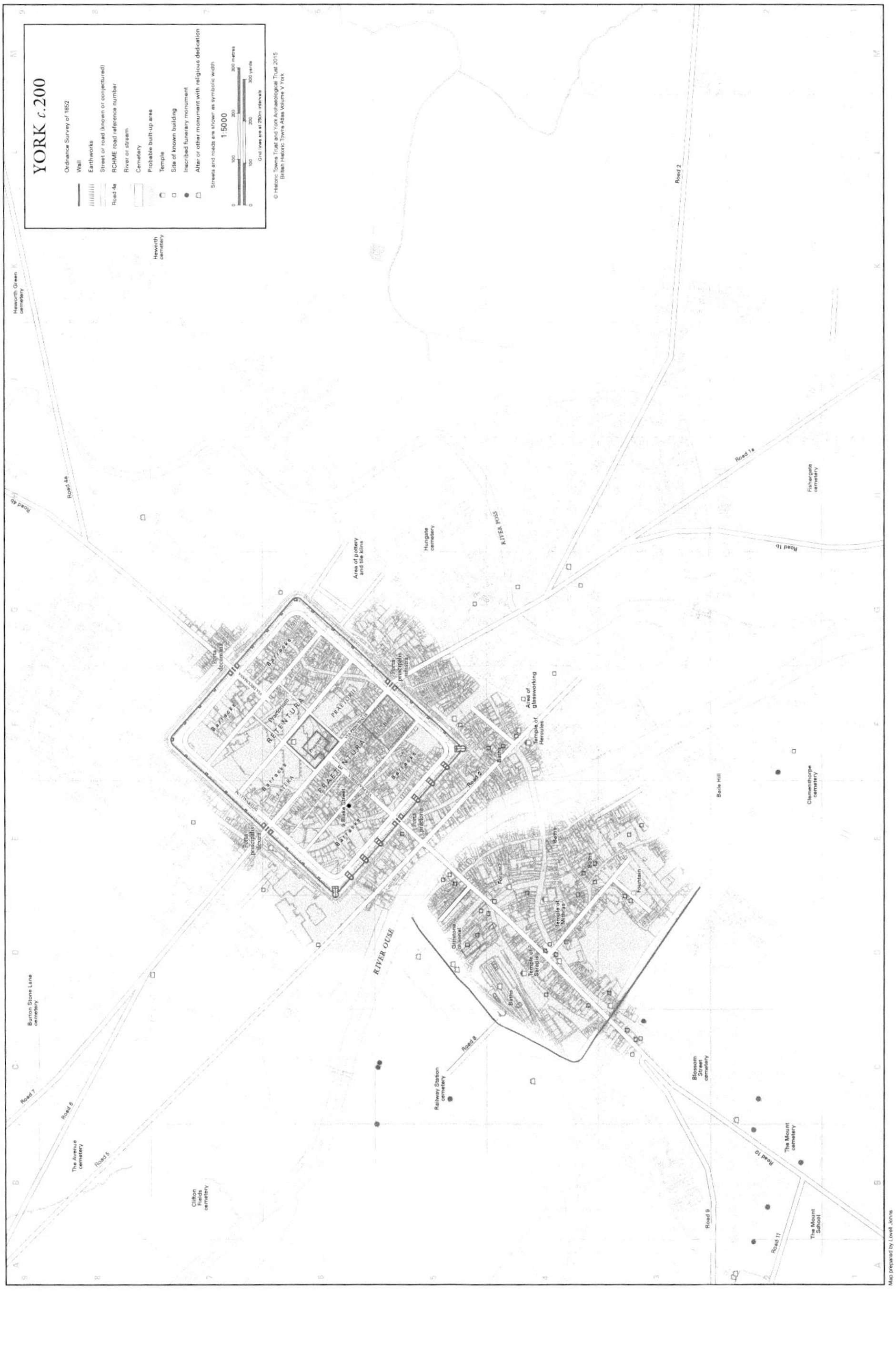

The extent of Roman York at the turn of the third century AD, showing the position and size of the fortress (red), settlement areas (brown) and cemeteries (green). (Reproduced with permission from the *British Historic Towns Atlas*, Volume V (ed. Peter Addyman), published by the Historic Towns Trust and York Archaeological Trust, 2015)

Indeed, because the city itself is such a wonderful place for history and heritage, our actual ability to reach down into Roman archaeological layers underground is often, quite rightly, prevented by the important historical nature of the remains above them. This is the case for most cities with a continuous history of occupation from the Roman period through to the modern day; we are left with a view into *Eboracum* akin to looking out of a cracked and murky window – the general picture makes sense and many points are brighter than others, but there are pieces that we cannot see because our view is physically blocked. However, this is not a cause for concern. Our understanding of the remains, and my ability to write this very book, is dependent upon the excellent work of a select few pioneers of the city's archaeology, upon whose giant shoulders we are standing.

Pioneers of Roman York

I have selected a short roll-call of five pioneers, though many others could well be mentioned.

Francis Drake (1696–1771)
Not the famous adventurer and sailor, this Francis Drake was a surgeon whose leisure time was spent in the pursuit of history and who was the first big name in Roman York. He personally inspected the many ancient monuments of York and was commissioned for £50 in 1731 by the city corporation to produce plans and maps of them. His great work was titled *Eboracum: The History and Antiquities of the City of York, from its Original to the Present Time together with the History of the Cathedral Church and the Lives of the Archbishops*. Coming in at 800 pages, Drake's *Eboracum* sought to write the first definitive history of the city, drawing upon some previous work by other antiquarians.

Revd Charles Wellbeloved (1769–1858)
One of the founders of the Yorkshire Philosophical Society in 1822 and honorary curator of antiquities in their museum (now the Yorkshire Museum) from its construction in 1830 until his death in 1858. His 1842 *Eburacum or York under the Romans* was the first

Portrait of Charles Wellbeloved, 1859. In the collection of York Art Gallery (YORAG: 1202). (©York Museums Trust (York Art Gallery) [CC BY-SA 4.0])

systematic account of Roman York, and this very book owes a great deal to Wellbeloved's endeavours. His museum guide, *Descriptive Accounts of the Antiquities in the Grounds and in the Museum of the Yorkshire Philosophical Society*, was first printed in 1852 and catalogued and discussed thousands of objects in the collection of the Yorkshire Museum.

Revd James Raine (1830–96)
Raine was chancellor of York Minster and an eminent archaeologist. Few Roman excavations took place in the latter half of the nineteenth century in York without the Reverend's personal interest. Importantly, he oversaw the excavation work undertaken in advance of the Victorian railway station – far and away York's most productive Roman site, which penetrated into a large swathe of a huge cemetery site on the south side of the River Ouse. In addition to writing a great number of publications and personal observations, he curated the antiquities in the Yorkshire Museum from 1873 until his death.

Leslie Peter Wenham (1911–90)
Wenham was an archaeologist and lecturer in history at St John's College, York (and later, the head of the department). He was an utterly prolific excavator in York in the 1950s, '60s and '70s and an editor of the *Yorkshire Archaeological Journal*. He is perhaps most notable for the extensive excavations of Trentholme Drive Roman cemetery.

Elizabeth Hartley (1947–2018)
Liz Hartley was the Keeper of Archaeology at the Yorkshire Museum for more than thirty years and developed several major exhibitions which helped to put York on the map as a place to see Roman archaeology. While the collection was very similar to that curated by Wellbeloved and then Raine a century earlier, she was able to help bring our understanding of it into the twentieth and then twenty-first century.

Elizabeth Hartley at the opening of a new Roman exhibition in the Yorkshire Museum in the 1980s. (Image from the Yorkshire Museum archive)

Early *Eboracum*

One of the earliest historical descriptions of the island of Britain comes to us from the writings of the great geographer Strabo at the start of the first century AD:

> Britain is triangular in shape... Most of the island is flat and overgrown with forests, although many of its districts are hilly. It bears grain, cattle, gold, silver, and iron. These things, accordingly, are exported from the island, as also hides, and slaves, and dogs that are by nature suited to the purposes of the chase.
>
> The men of Britain are taller than the Celti, and not so yellow-haired, although their bodies are of looser build... I myself, in Rome, saw mere lads towering as much as half a foot above the tallest people in the city, although they were bandy-legged and presented no fair lines anywhere else in their figure...
>
> For the purposes of war they use chariots for the most part...Their weather is more rainy than snowy; and on the days of clear sky fog prevails so long a time that throughout a whole day the sun is to be seen for only three or four hours around about midday.
>
> [Strabo, *Geography*, Book IV, Chapter V]

A modern statue depicting the Greek geographer Strabo at Amasya (Turkey), where he was born. (©Zeynel Cebeci via Wikiema Commons [CC BY Attribution SA 4.0])

The latter paragraph, in particular, probably conjures a clear memory for anyone who has spent any amount of time in Britain. The remainder is a reference to the pre-Roman inhabitants of Britain and the value of both people and their land. Prior to the arrival of the Roman armies, Britain was in the period commonly referred to as the 'Iron Age'. Iron Age peoples were loosely grouped into large populations or tribes, the names of which we hear about from coins and the surviving texts of a number of Roman writers. For example, the Iceni, the Catuvellauni, or the Brigantes may be familiar names.

Julius Caesar undertook a brief military expedition to Britain in 55–54 BC and chronicled his campaigns alongside producing general notes on the landscape, the people and the customs he encountered in *De Bello Gallico* (the Gallic Wars). The impact of the Caesarian expedition on York is minimal as the campaign was brief and never intended to get further than the south-east part of Britain. In his 1906 guidebook to the history of York city, G. A. Auden put it succinctly: 'In considering the subjugation of Britain by the Romans, we may dismiss the punitive expeditions undertaken by Julius Caesar with a mere passing notice.' Caesar's British legacy is historically important, but not directly applicable to a discussion of archaeology in the north of Britain.

AD 43, though, was a hugely important date in the history of Britain, heralding the arrival of over 20,000 Roman soldiers tasked by the Emperor Claudius with expanding the territory of the Roman Empire and gaining an important military victory to secure his claim to the Imperial title. For the purposes of this book, a blow-by-blow account of the Roman invasion period is unnecessary and has been tackled by much more learned

The Walkington hoard of Iron Age coins, dating to AD 0–50. The names of tribes were often written on such coins and they could be traded all over Britain. In the Yorkshire Museum (YORYM: 2005.2202). (©York Museums Trust (Yorkshire Museum) [CC BY-SA 4.0])

Marble bust of Gaius Julius Caesar in the Musei Vaticani, Rome. (Public Domain via Wikimedia Commons)

scholars in the past. Britain would certainly have teased the economic sweet-tooth of the Roman world, offering mineral wealth, land for development and a total population estimated at around 500,000–1,000,000 people – potential allies, potential tax payers, and potential slaves for the Roman Empire.

After the invasion of AD 43 it took an entire generation for the Roman military to arrive at the site of York. In the mid-first century AD much of the area of North Yorkshire was under the control of the Brigantes, an Iron Age tribe whose lands extended across much of northern Britain. Their queen, Cartimandua, was friendly to the Roman invaders and acted as a 'client-queen' – her lands were left free in return for loyalty to Rome. For capturing Caratacus (the figurehead of the anti-Roman faction during the invasion period) the Roman writer Tacitus recorded that Cartimandua was given great wealth by Rome.

The Brigantes eventually gained a reputation for civil unrest and revolt, but all-out war between Rome and the tribes of the North in the middle of the first century was

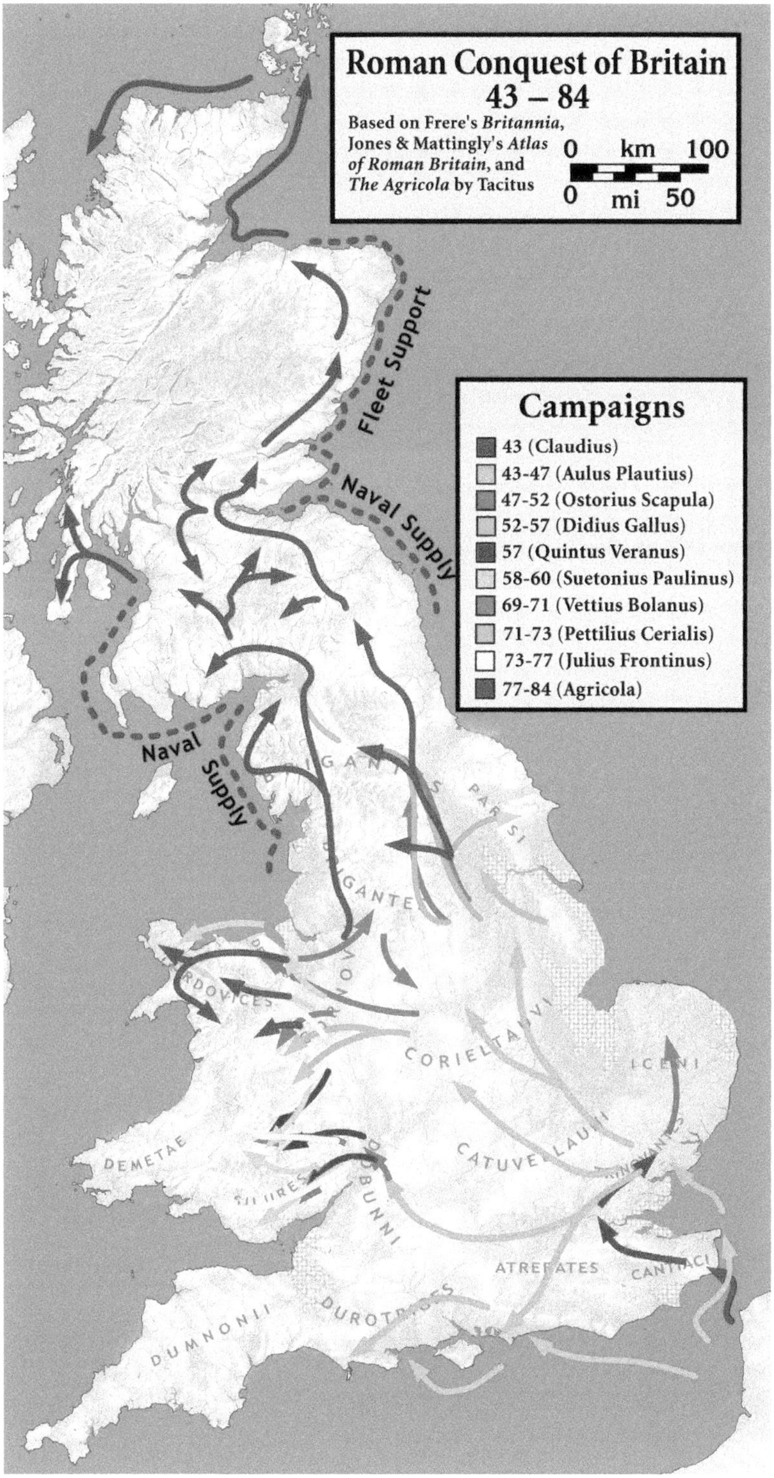

A map of the invasion of Roman Britain. (©Wikimedia Commons [CC BY-SA 3.0])

A figurine depicting a horned deity from Aldborough, the capital city of the Brigantes and seat of power for Cartimandua. In the Yorkshire Museum (YORYM: H2400). (©York Museums Trust (Yorkshire Museum) [CC BY-SA 4.0])

certainly delayed, if not prevented, by the relationship between Cartimandua and the Roman governors of Britain. This was not to last. In AD 57, Cartimandua divorced her husband Venutius and instead took his armour-bearer, Vellocatus, as her husband. Venutius began an uprising against the queen and eventually against the Roman Army in the region. This first rebellion was defeated by the *Legio IX Hispana,* 9th 'Hispanic' Legion, but Venutius remained alive. In AD 69 Venutius again rebelled, causing Cartimandua to appeal to the Roman government for help – the army managed to evacuate her from the area after which no more is heard of the queen in the historic records.

This political upheaval and the continuing anti-Roman sentiment of Venutius caused the establishment of a permanent military garrison in the area and this historical background was the genesis of the city of York. AD 70/71 is the year that the city was established as a Roman fortress, but it was a reaction to a political issue rather than a carefully considered choice by the Roman Army. The site chosen was a plateau at the confluence of the River Foss and the River Ouse, which is navigable by boat all the way to the coast. This site is also situated near to a probable tribal centre of the Brigantes at Aldborough (30 miles to the north-west) and near to the tribal lands of the Parisi – the other, smaller, Iron Age population in the area, based in East Yorkshire. From this point onwards, a series of campaigns were launched against the Brigantes, initially by the then Governor of the province, Petilius Cerialis (Governor, AD 71–4).

> But when Vespasian [AD 69], in the course of his general triumph, restored stable government to Britain, there came a succession of great generals and splendid armies, and the hopes of our enemies dwindled. Petilius Cerialis at once struck terror into the hearts by attacking the state of the Brigantes, which is said to be the most populous in the whole province. After a series of battles – some of them by no means bloodless – Petilius had overrun, if not actually conquered, the major part of their territory...”
>
> (Tacitus, *Agricola*, XVII)

The first few years of the city of York's history were, no doubt, covered in blood – *Eboracum* as it came to be known would have been the launch pad, supply depot and HQ for this active military campaign. The name is a Latinisation of a Brittonic word meaning 'yew tree place'. Unlike many of the other Roman towns, York was never a big Iron Age centre. Only sporadic evidence is available to suggest that this area of land between the rivers Ouse and Foss was used very much at all before the Roman arrival here.

The very first fortress was laid out in AD 70/71 by the retinue of military surveyors and engineers who formed part of every Roman legion. A fortress is traditionally a 'playing card' shape – longer on its north–south axis than its east–west axis. The fortress at York can be quite accurately measured to a size of 1,600 x 1,360 *pes montalis*. A *pes* is a Roman foot, equivalent to 0.971 of an Imperial British foot (or 29.6 cm). The *pes* was an officially regulated measurement, based on a single ruler housed in the Temple of Juno Moneta in Rome. A right angle is created through an application

The Emperor Vespasian depicted on a coin from the Binnington Carr hoard, dating to AD 77–78. In the Yorkshire Museum (YORYM: 2000.1988). (©York Museums Trust (Yorkshire Museum) [CC BY-SA 4.0])

of Pythagoras's Theorem and the careful geometric planning of a well-organised and experienced surveying team in order to create the fortress shape. From these measurements a maximum size for the fortress enclosure wall of 473 m x 402 m can thus be calculated. The original surveying principles used for the first fortress of AD 70/71 were adhered to for at least 150 years after its construction, with necessary rebuilding and repairs staying true to the original plan. A large proportion of the commercial and tourism enterprises of modern day York are contained within or immediately beyond this original rectangular boundary.

The labour force for this construction, initially in timber, was the legionaries themselves. The Roman legion was a multi-functional creature; many soldiers had additional trades or skills to apply to a major construction programme – the masons, bricklayers, carpenters, lumberjacks and ditch-diggers who built *Eboracum* were all legionary soldiers on temporary secondment.

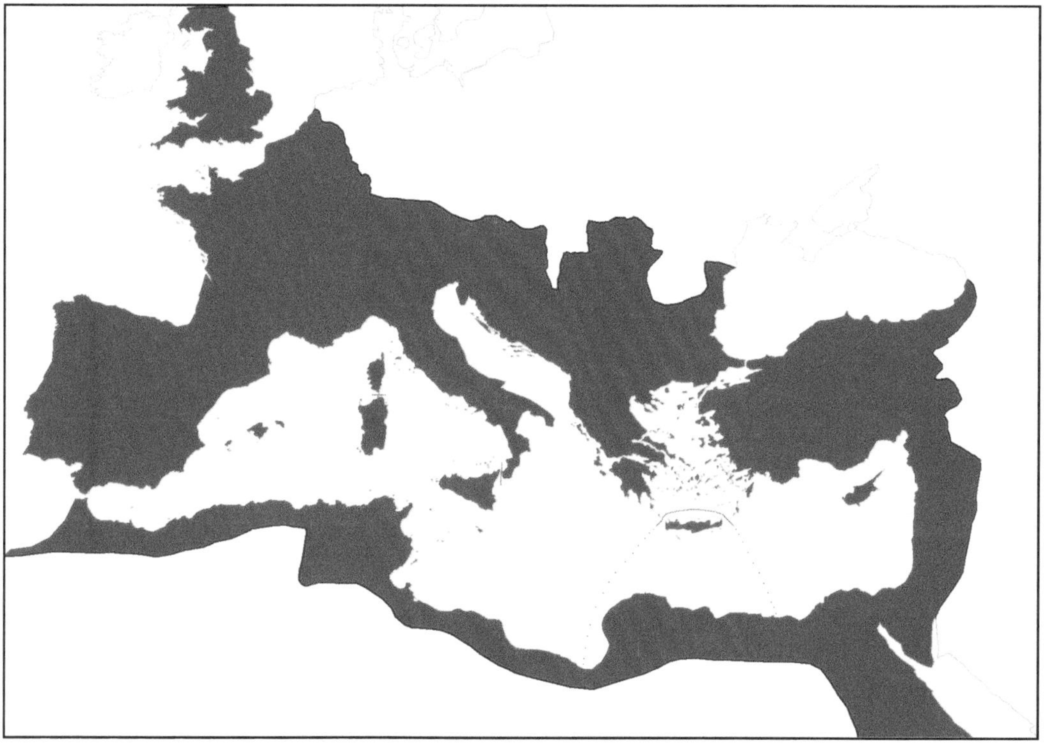

The extent of the Roman Empire. (©Public Domain via Wikimedia Commons)

The Eagle's Fortress

Fortress Layout

Much of our understanding of the physical makeup of the fortress at *Eboracum* is, unhelpfully, guesswork based on the pattern of military buildings seen elsewhere in Roman Britain and the Empire. Roman structural remains are very difficult to access in central York, largely because of the success of the city and its development into an important early medieval and medieval centre. Excavations in York were frequently undertaken in basements and cellars, which already penetrated to the depths of several metres usually required to encounter such remains.

At its core, a legionary fortress was a monumental structure indeed. A level of standardisation of building formats and architectural technique within the Roman Army resulted in very similar structures across the Empire. Each individual fort had its own structural nuances which developed over time, but as a starting point a series of major buildings would be expected to be found within every fortress.

A legionary fortress was, at its core, a huge camp designed to house soldiers. Excavations in 1975 by York Archaeological Trust established that there were multiple periods of rebuilding and reuse of the barracks, starting from the first-century timber buildings (constructed by the 9th Legion) through their rebuilding in stone in the mid-second century, and onto the latest phases of Roman military occupation of the buildings. The barrack spaces were simple structures with squat rectangular rooms designed to hold a *contuburnium* ('tent-group') of eight soldiers sleeping in bunks. The end block of each row was for the use of the centurion. Only fragments of these barracks have been located but their format is so standardised that the presumed location of the full complement can be extrapolated with some accuracy. The barracks occupied the northern and southern thirds of the fort.

The central third is the logistics and command hub of the fortress, surrounded by the barracks on two sides, containing at least the *principia* (HQ building), the *praetorium* (the commander's house), *horrea* (granaries) and the *valetudinarium* (the hospital). *Principiae* are commonly found as a large open-courtyard building surrounded by small rooms – offices, where the administrators of the army greased the bureaucratic wheels of the legion. This building was kept at the very heart of the fortress and it should come as no surprise that it has remained at the very heart of modern day York.

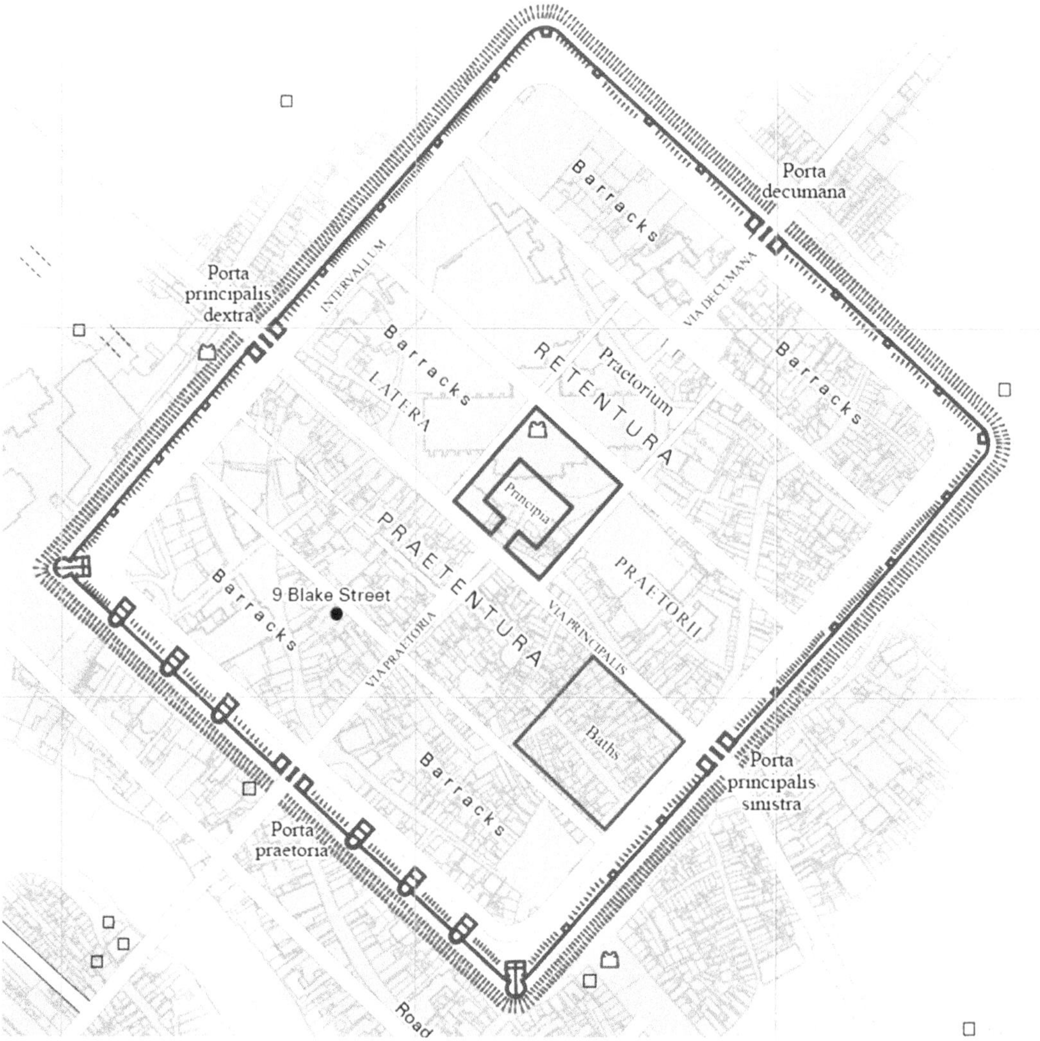

Plan of the fortress. (Reproduced with permission from the *British Historic Towns Atlas*, Volume V (ed. Peter Addyman), published by the Historic Towns Trust and York Archaeological Trust, 2015)

At the rear of the *principia* was a *basilica*. The first stone *basilica*, dating from the late first/early second century AD, was a monumentally huge building for the period. It has been described as 'cathedral-like in scale', measuring 65.8 m in length and 22.6 m in width. It had two internal colonnades, entirely unique to this building. The vast majority of the *principia* has not been excavated at York but the *basilica* was discovered as part of important work to the foundations directly below York Minster (York's huge medieval cathedral) between 1966 and 1973. Small fragments of the structure remain on public display in the Undercroft gallery within the Minster itself. To help demonstrate the monstrous size of this building, which would have loomed large over much of the fortress, a column from the *basilica* has been re-erected outside of the Minster and acts

The re-erected *basilica* column, now on public display outside of York Minster. (©Carole Raddato via Wikimedia Commons [CC BY-Attribution SA 2.0])

as a sense of scale for the size of the Roman building, standing 7.8 m high. This was probably the tallest building in the north of Roman Britain for a long time afterwards.

Being the man in charge of the 5,000 soldiers in a fortress came with some perks, notably the use of one of the largest structures so far uncovered from Roman York. The *praetorium* was a private house solely for use by the legate (*legatus* – 'legionary commander'), his family and his slaves. It was a seat of power within the seat of power and senior officers, officials, guests, friends and family visiting the commander would have been wined and dined here.

All of these structures were encased within a huge defensive wall. The walls of the later medieval town were constructed over the Roman walls, so while much of the physical remains are no longer visible, their approximate footprint is. The modern city wall is a major tourist attraction and thousands of visitors to York 'walk the walls' every year – they are walking around the approximate line of the Roman wall and doing so is the best way to get a sense of the scale of Roman York.

The fortress itself was the first area to be properly defended. The first phase (AD 71–4) of defences consisted of an earth bank with a turf front and a wooden palisade above it. A ditch beyond this, known informally as an 'ankle breaker', served a defensive

The south-west bastion tower of the fortress of *Eburacum*, known as the Multangular Tower. Approximately the lower half of this is Roman; the upper half was rebuilt in the Middle Ages. (Public Domain (ChrisO) via Wikimedia Commons)

function as well as facilitating drainage. This wall was rebuilt to a height of at least 3 m, being 6 m wide at the base. Steps were presumably placed at intervals around the interior to allow access a wall-walk above the rampart.

By about AD 108, in the reign of the Emperor Trajan, the timber fortress had started to be rebuilt in stone. This project was a massive undertaking and would have required at least 48,000 cubic metres of building stone – recent research suggests that this probably took decades to complete. The walls on the south side of the river, those surrounding the civilian settlements, have not been as comprehensively studied as those in the north, but also show that much of the medieval walls were built above a Roman stone wall.

The well-known Multangular Tower is one of the few structural pieces of Roman York visible today in the city. Housed in the Museum Gardens, the tower was the south-western bastion tower of the original fortress. It projects beyond the city wall, stands to a height of 9.1 m and there are ten sides visible, based on a fourteen-sided polygon. Although previously thought to date to the fourth century, recent reassessments suggest that it dates from the late second or early third century instead. The tower is south-facing, looking over the River Ouse towards the civilian settlement across it, and would have been only one of a great number of interval towers spanning the walls of the Roman fortress.

A Soldier's Job

When the fortress was first constructed, the Roman military was broadly split up between two major groups: the legionaries and the auxiliaries. Both are professional soldiers, but were categorised by very different legal parameters. A legionary was a free Roman citizen, recruited under the age of forty-five, enlisted in the army for a period of twenty-five years, and organised into legions of 5,000–6,000 men. An auxiliary was, legally, a non-citizen, recruited to fight in the support wing of the Roman Army (throughout the first three centuries AD) and eventually rewarded with citizenship for himself and his children after twenty-five years of service. Auxiliaries were organised into units called *cohors* (cohorts) or *alae* (wings) of *c.* 500 men. It is a fallacy to think that all Roman soldiers were from Rome or, indeed, from Italy. Research has shown that in the first half of the first century AD, nearly 65 per cent of Roman legionaries were recruited from Italy, which had reduced dramatically to less than 1 per cent by the second century – Roman soldiers were a diverse bunch, recruited from all over. It has been estimated that in the early second century AD the whole of the Roman Army, spread cross the whole Empire, included a total of 155,000 Legionaries and 218,000 auxiliaries.

The original invasion force of AD 43 included four legions, totalling approximately 20,000–25,000 soldiers. The four were each based in a purpose-built fortress, the auxilia that accompanied them were housed in much smaller forts – all constructed by the soldiers themselves. York was a legionary fortress and thus housed 5,000–6,000 legionaries at its capacity. The 9th Legion were based in York from AD 70 and eventually replaced by the 6th Legion from the AD 120s onwards – so York had two different units living in it over its lifetime.

The day-to-day life of a Roman legionary in the garrison was fairly uneventful. Guard duty on the walls, towers, gates, and sentry duty for the legate or in the headquarters

Re-enactor dressed as a legionary. (©MatthiasKabel [CC BY-Attribution SA 3.0])

would take up a regular chunk of time in a soldier's life. Records from elsewhere in the Empire suggest that of a unit in Syria of 800 men, 20 per cent undertook guard duty every 24 hours; 120 men a day. Scaling these numbers directly to a legion of 6,000 soldiers would suggest 1,200 men undertook a watch every day. Other duties, as well as the trades mentioned, included patrols, detached duties and parades; these on top of the mundane routines of training, cleaning and cooking.

A military organisation as huge as this one was fuelled by bureaucracy. The Roman writer Polybius records that passwords for guards were regularly changed and new ones written on tablets and passed to the sentries by an officer. The rare survival of such wooden tablets at the fort of Vindolanda on the Hadrianic Frontier has shown that the army produced thousands of reports, orders, lists and other miscellaneous correspondences throughout its life. Many of these would be burnt or thrown away – at which point only very specific archaeological conditions would preserve them for future study. York has no such evidence yet, but the literate tools to produce an endless supply of administrative information have – three *styli* from Blake Street, within the fortress, take the form of a thin metal cylinder with a point at one end (in the general form of a modern pen) used to scratch notes into a wax tablet. The other tip of these *styli* is a small, flat spatula used, warmed up, to erase the notes in wax so that it could be re-used. The Vindolanda tablets have shown that a Roman military unit was not always at full strength, with soldiers seconded to other forts and installations or duties with the governor, away on recreational leave, or sick or injured. Vindolanda Tablet 154 recorded that of a listed full strength of 752, only 265 were physically available in the fort for active duty at that time. The same must also have been true for the garrison at *Eboracum* – rarely would the unit be at absolute capacity within the fortress walls in the day-to-day execution of its duties.

Individual soldiers and their stories are very difficult to find in the archaeological record, even with the excellent preservation at York and the substantial excavation of cemetery sites. Thankfully, from the tombstone evidence at York we can name at least a few of its original inhabitants:

Lucius Duccius Rufinus, standard-bearer of the 9th Legion.
[Gaius?], son of Caius, of the 9th Legion.
Lucius Celerinius Vitalis, staff clerk of the 9th Legion
Marcus Minuciius Audenus, soldier of the 6th Legion.
Claudius Hieronymianus, legate of the 6th Legion.
Caeresius [August]inus, veteran of the 6th Legion.
Felicius Simplex of the 6th Legion.
Aurelius Super, centurion of the 6th Legion.
Gaius Aeresius Saenus, veteran of the 6th Legion.
Manlius Crescens, veteran of the 6th Legion.
Lucius Bebius Crescens, soldier of the 6th Legion.
Antonius Gargilianus, prefect of the 6th Legion.
Septimius Lupianus, centurion.
Mar[cus] Vitalis, centurion.
Claudius Florentius, decurion.
Publius Aelius Marcianus, prefect of the cohort.

The physical presence of soldiers at York is otherwise attested by the few fragments of metalwork that we can associate with their profession. A small number of sword fragments, arrowheads, ballista bolt tips, ballista balls and lead shot are some of the weapons which have survived. It is perhaps surprising that more weapons have not been discovered in the fortress, but soldiers were not often considered wasteful. Most weapons are large, conspicuous, quite difficult to lose during their working lifetime and (perhaps most importantly archaeologically) are made of iron and liable to corrode beyond recognition underground. Fragments of armour, harness fittings and decorative pendants have also survived. Perhaps the most impressive of these is a belt fitting, broadly rectangular in shape but with inwardly curving sides. The flat face of the copper alloy plate is inlaid with hundreds of exceptionally tiny tesserae, or coloured squares, to create a decorative mosaic panel. A central roundel has alternating panels of nine-square grids of blue and white or red and white squares, each square no more

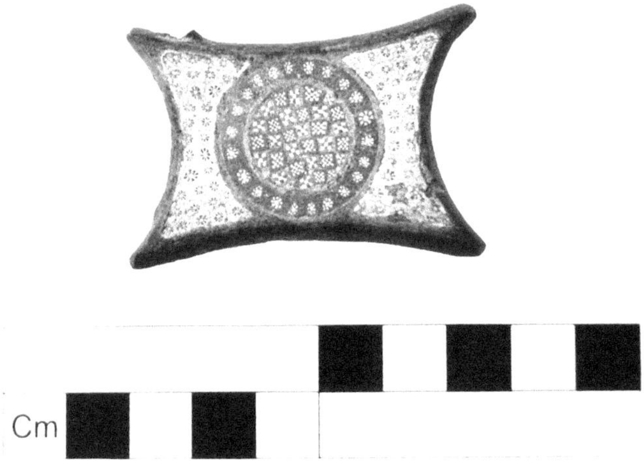

Millefiori belt plate from Blake Street. In the Yorkshire Museum (YORYM: 1975.6.496). (©York Museums Trust (Yorkshire Museum) [CC BY-SA 4.0])

than 0.5 mm wide, surrounded by a thick blue enamel border. The border is inset with radiate white flowers. The flanks of the panel are white/cream in colour and decorated with blue flowers instead. This technique is called millefiori – it is a testament to the skill of a Roman craftsperson as well as the fashion sense of a garrison legionary.

Until the third century AD, Roman soldiers were forbidden from legally marrying while serving with the army, but it was to be expected that non-legally binding 'de facto marriage' partnerships grew up between soldiers and women. It is an important distinction to make as this legal relationship affected the rights of any children from the relationship. Officially, all children born to non-legally married soldiers were illegitimate. However, if the soldier and spouse were both Roman citizens (an important legal position), the child would also be a Roman citizen and protected by the judicial systems of the Roman Empire. The child of a mother who was not a citizen would also not be a citizen and was thus unable to inherit any property from the father. It is unclear how many soldiers did form such unions over time.

A small amount of tombstone evidence does record some of the relationships between soldiers and their families. For example, a centurion of the 6th Legion named Aurelius Superus died aged thirty-eight and was buried in a huge stone sarcophagus with an inscription commissioned by his wife, Aurelia. The sarcophagus burial tradition became popular in the third and fourth centuries – this text thus came after the legalisation of marriage. A particularly poignant memorial to a lost daughter was installed by Felicius Simplex, another soldier of the 6th Legion:

DM SIMPLICIAE FLORENTINE
ANIME INNOCENTISSIME
QVE VIXIT MENSES DECEM
FELICIVS SIMPLEX PATER FECIT
LEG VI V

The text reads: 'To the shades of the departed, and Simplicia Florentina, a most innocent soul. She died aged ten months. Felicius Simplex, her father and solider of the 6th Legion, built this.' This sorrowful tombstone constructed by a mourning father highlights that

The sarcophagus of Simplicia Florentina. The Mount, 1838. In the Yorkshire Museum (YORYM: 2003.4). (©York Museums Trust (Yorkshire Museum) [CC BY-SA 4.0])

the military in Roman York should not been seen simply as professional soldiers stationed at a frontier outpost – there are personal stories which survive that highlight aspects of the human experience felt by those in York nearly two millennia ago.

The Ninth Legion

Eboracum was home to only two different legions throughout its four-century history. The establishment, initial construction and laying out of the fortress was undertaken by the 9th 'Hispanic' Legion (*Legio Nones Hispana*) in AD 70/71. The 9th were involved in all the major campaigns of the Roman invasion period, though were very nearly destroyed during the Boudiccan Revolt.

There are two objects in the Yorkshire Museum which help illuminate the story of the 9th Legion in York. The first is a huge tombstone, dedicated to Lucius Duccius Rufinus. The stone is carved from local limestone, stands nearly 2 metres tall and shows Lucius in his off-duty military garb. The inscription beneath reads:

L DVCCIUS
L VOLT RUFI
NVS VIEN
SIGNIF LEG VIIII
AN XXIIX
HSE

The tombstone of Lucius Duccius Rufinus, standard bearer of the 9th Legion. In the Yorkshire Museum (YORYM: 1998.19). (©York Museums Trust (Yorkshire Museum) [CC BY-SA 4.0])

The translation of this text reveals a great deal about the life of Lucius: 'Lucius Duccius Rufinus, Son of Lucius, of the Voltrini voting tribe, from Vienne, standard-bearer of the 9th Legion, aged 28 lies buried here.' Lucius was a legionary of the 9th Legion, a standard-bearer: a role requiring the safe keeping of the unit's standard (a pole with the unit's insignia and awards) and the pay box. Vienne is in modern-day Belgium, but the three names displayed on the tombstone (the *tria nomina*) identifies Lucius as a full Roman citizen. He died in service of his legion at York and was buried in a cemetery to the south of the site with this huge stone commemorating his memory. It is quite poignant to consider that one of the additional roles of the standard-bearer was to collect a small payment from each soldier, out of his wages, into a 'burial fund' to ensure his comrades could afford a suitable tombstone upon the unfortunate event of their death. Rufinus was thus responsible for looking after the contributions that, ultimately, may have paid for this very stone monument. Twenty-eight years of age is quite young for a soldier to have passed away and the temptation may be to assume he lost his life in battle; however, if this was the case he is less likely to have been brought back to the fortress for proper burial. The three letters HSE at the lowest edge of the inscription are an abbreviation of *Hic Situs Est* (literally: 'he lies here'). I suggest that Lucius is more likely to have succumbed to disease or infection than a heroic death in battle, but that this highlights the ever-present risks of a military career in the first century AD.

A second inscription in the Yorkshire Museum is particularly interesting in the history of the 9th Legion as it records the latest inscription dateable to their time in York. This inscription is a dedication stone – a plaque erected on a building to record its construction, listing the reigning Emperor and all of his worldly titles. Only the central third has survived, but a sound expansion of the full inscription is possible. Dating quite firmly to AD 108, the inscription reads:

IMP CAESAR
DIVI NERVAE FIL NERVA
TRAIANVS AVG GERM DAC
IVS PONTIFEX MAXIMVS TRIBV
NICIAE POTESTATIS XII IMP V COS V PP
PORTAM PER LEG VIIII HISP FECIT

The first five lines of this inscription are merely an introduction to the name of the Emperor Trajan and his full honours. To translate: 'The Emperor Caesar Nerva Trajan Augustus, son of the deified Nerva, Conqueror of Germany, Conqueror of Dacia, pontifex maximus, in his twelfth year of tribunician power, six times acclaimed *imperator*, five times consul, father of his country, built this gate by agency of the Ninth Hispanic Legion.' Recording the reconstruction of a gateway (probably in stone),

The reconstructed building inscription of the 9th Legion from Kings Square, York. In the Yorkshire Museum (YORYM: 1998.21). (©York Museums Trust (Yorkshire Museum) [CC BY-SA 4.0])

this inscription was located in King's Square, adjacent to the original east gateway of the fortress (the *porta principalis dextra*). The list of titles given to Trajan allows us to firmly date this to AD 108. At some point between AD 108 and AD 120, the 9th Legion leaves York and the 6th Legion takes its place. This change, and the comparative quietening of the 9th Legion's archaeological footprint, is taken to suggest that it was destroyed by enemy action at some point. Previous thought focussed on its potential destruction here in Britain, or even at York. A short passage of text from Marcus Cornelius Fronto, writing in the AD 160s, who wrote to the Emperor Marcus Aurelius is often taken as evidence of a great military loss between AD 117–122: 'Indeed, when your grandfather Hadrian held Imperial power, what great numbers of soldiers were killed [in Jerusalem], what great numbers by the Britons.'

While the mystery surrounding these events inspired a famous fictional story (Rosemary Sutcliffe's 1954 adventure the *Eagle of the Ninth*, recently inspiring Hollywood to create 2011's *The Eagle*), a small amount of archaeological evidence suggests that the 9th left Britain entirely and were garrisoned for a time at Nijmegen (Netherlands) before moving on to Parthia, where they may have later been destroyed. The painful reality is that we don't know yet and can't make a conclusive argument until more information is gathered and new finds come to light.

The Sixth Legion

The fortunes of the 6th Legion and that of York are intimately entwined. In the early part of the second century, the 9th Legion was replaced at York by the 6th Victorious Legion (*Legio Sextes Victrix*). The 6th was responsible for much of the rebuilding of the fortress in stone, was seconded to construct large portions of Hadrian's Wall in the AD 120s, and remained the garrisoned unit at *Eboracum* until the very end of the Roman period in Britain in the fifth century AD. It is the 6th Legion that really defines the military history of Roman York. The 6th Legion was based in York for *c.* 270 years between AD 120 and AD 410 – generations of legionaries who were part of the 6th lived, worked, retired and died in York.

In AD 122, large detachments (*vexilatio*) of the 6th Legion were seconded to the northern frontier of Britain to begin construction of Hadrian's Wall, the great linear barrier running the narrowest width of Roman Britain along the Tyne–Solway isthmus. Construction was undertaken between AD 122 and AD 126 and it is likely that large sections of the garrison were away for years at a time. *Eboracum*'s garrison would have been on a skeleton staff throughout this period, presumably rotating troops between the frontier and the fortress seasonally. The 6th were joined by the 2nd and 20th legions in constructing Hadrian's Wall, all of whom left their mark on the Wall. Literally. There are several building inscriptions recording the finished sections of wall by the legion, or a specific cohort or century from it – we know the 6th were involved in building projects north of York at Chesters Fort, South Shields, and Piercebridge.

An inscription from Newcastle even mentions seconded sections of all three legions working on a single project. The legionaries were never responsible for garrisoning the Wall itself, merely building it. After the wall was finished, several years were spent back in garrison before the 6th was called north to build again. The construction of the Antonine Wall along the Forth–Clyde isthmus in Scotland was begun in AD 142.

Marks of the legions: tile stamps from York bearing the abbreviated names of the 9th and 6th Legions. In the Yorkshire Museum (YORYM: 1973.1.11 & 2012.564). (©York Museums Trust (Yorkshire Museum) [CC BY-SA 4.0])

Due to the sheer length of service that the 6th held at York, they have left a much larger archaeological imprint. As well as legionaries, the epigraphic record tells us about centurions and even the legate. The legate was the commander of the legion, a position held by the rich and powerful, usually as part of a political career – during the various civil wars of the Roman Empire many legionary legates themselves became Emperor; Vespasian and Septimius Severus were both famous military commanders before they became Emperors. Claudius Hieronymanius is the only legate of the garrison at York named on stone, from the very early part of the third century, but was one in a long line of upper-class citizens who held the job. The legate had a huge private house in the centre of the fortress, where he resided with his family and slaves.

Inscription recording the construction of a temple to the god Sol by a detachment of the 6th Legion, in Corbridge, Northumberland. (©Alun Salt via Wikimedia Commons [CC BY-Attribution SA 2.0])

He'd have the job of entertaining important or high-ranking guests to the city as well as acting as the signatory of the huge administration system required to run a group of 6,000 professional soldiers, and was answerably only to the Governor of the province.

Finishing a career in the Roman Army did not necessarily mean leaving York and travelling elsewhere – we know that many soldiers were granted land or money and some used this to stay in York. Gaius Aeresius Saenus and Manlius Crescens are both named on inscriptions as veterans of the 6th Legion. Gaius set up a tombstone, rather tragically, to his wife Flavia and both a young daughter and son. Auxilia from the region were granted a 'military diploma' upon their completion of service – an important document that granted them the rights of Roman citizen. Veterans of long service and, perhaps, discharge through injury, of both auxilia and the legions would have been clearly present in the community of Roman York.

A military diploma awarded to an auxiliary soldier upon completion of his term of service. Brompton-by-Sawdon, North Yorkshire, 2008. In the Yorkshire Museum (YORYM: 2008.171). (©York Museums Trust (Yorkshire Museum) [CC BY-SA 4.0])

Across the River

The military establishment that was '*Eboracum* – the fortress' was by no means all of the built landscape of ancient York. The large military forces of the Roman world came with attachments, even in its mobile stages, of a baggage train of non-essential military personnel in addition to the hangers-on, tradespeople, guides, etc., that made up this varied and fluctuating group of people. These folk may have been 'official' or entirely unofficial and present for their own reasons. Largely this group remains invisible in the archaeological record, given the transience that may have naturally marked their working lives. The point is that the fortress, shortly after its inception, was the centre of development for a sprawling civilian settlement, eventually bigger in geographical size (and maybe even population) than the fortress itself; the two were symbiotic and the fortunes of one certainly affected the other. The previous chapter was an opportunity to discuss the physical remains within the fortress area and this complimentary introduction discusses the archaeology beyond the fortress.

From the earliest stages of *Eboracum*'s construction, a non-military encampment associated with the fortress was likely to have flourished. This civilian settlement established itself as a major component of the permanent inhabited landscape of Roman York, comprising an amorphous group of buildings which may be defined by function – housing and dwellings, shops, workshops, temples, warehouses and stores, and many other structures. The civilian establishment on the south side of the River Ouse, joined to the fortress by a bridge, was eventually awarded the municipal rank of *Colonia*, which bore its own rewards. Its original extent is relatively easy to identify as it was surrounded by a wall (on top of which the current city wall stands).

The civilian settlement would have been a busy, crowded place with substantial through-traffic both by foot and by vehicles. Workshops, houses and the large bathhouse would have constantly burned wood, making this area of York noisy, busy and probably sooty throughout. The main road leading through the centre would have been a focus for the shop fronts and mobile tradespeople selling, potentially, anything from meat and bread, sweet pastry snacks, shoes and furniture to jewellery, flowers, even slaves. The fortress proper was by no means a quiet place, but at its largest extent, this civilian part of *Eboracum*, with its many people undertaking the normal day-to-day activities of the period, would have been an assault on the senses and the focal point of the surrounding area. Access to the fortress was restricted, so the free-moving population, bolstered in numbers by the garrisoned soldiers allowed out of barracks, made the areas outside of the fortress the real place to be.

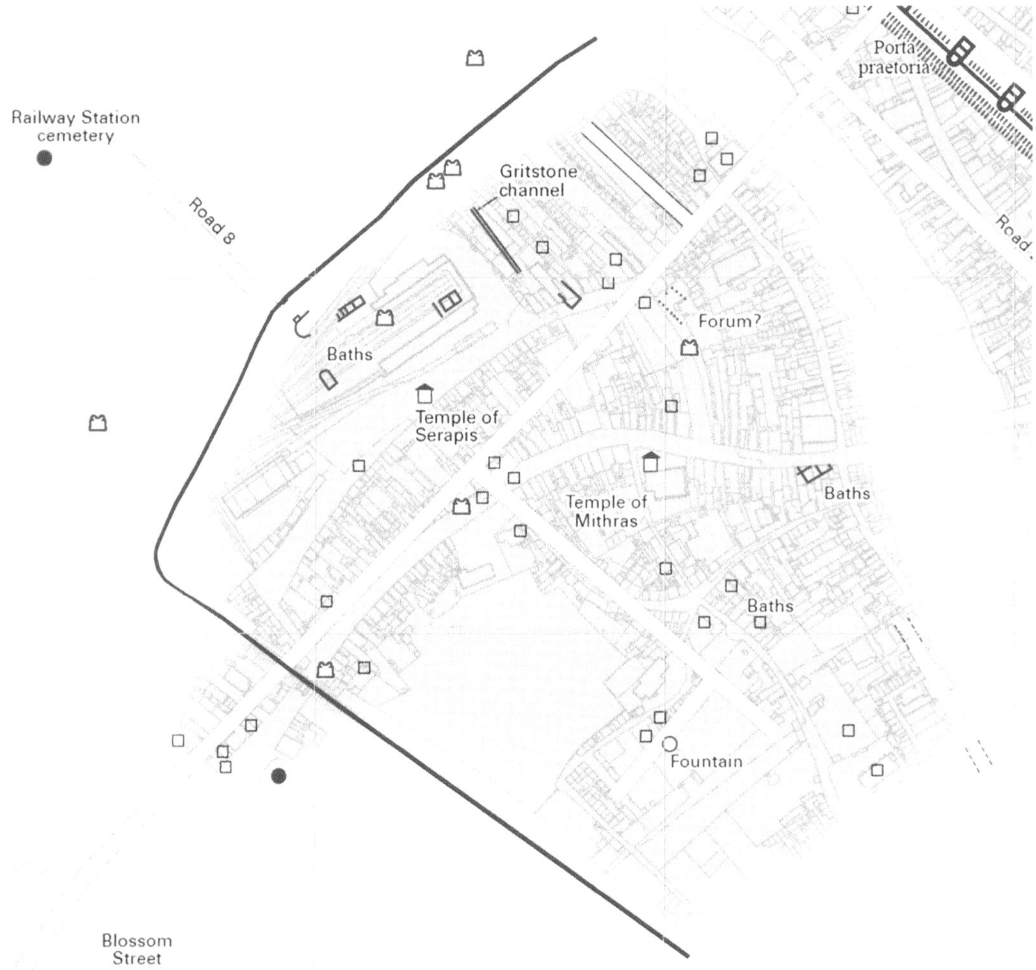

Buildings in the *Colonia*. (Reproduced with permission from the *British Historic Towns Atlas*, Volume V (ed. Peter Addyman), published by the Historic Towns Trust and York Archaeological Trust, 2015)

Defining a Colony

The '*Colonia*' status, literally translating as 'Colony', is a somewhat archaic term to be applied to the Roman settlement at York by the time it was formally given. Think of it as a mark of status, like the honorific title 'Royal' given to towns or boroughs in modern Britain. It is a phrase with its roots in the earlier days of the Roman Republic, where groups of citizens or military veterans formally colonised areas in the Mediterranean, but the Imperial use of this involved land grants to legionary veterans within the territories in which they were stationed. The '*Colonia*' title was an important honorific rank within the Roman Empire – only four other towns in Britain were granted the status (Colchester, Gloucester, Lincoln, and London). The exact date in which the civic rank of *Colonia* was bestowed upon *Eboracum* (thus creating the official name: *Colonia Eboracensis*) is unclear, though veterans would certainly have settled there from the early second century at the latest. The earliest dateable inscription which names *Eboracum* as a colony is AD 237 and comes from Bordeaux – from an altar given in thanks for a safe sea crossing from its patron and York resident, the priest Marcus Aurelius Lunaris. It is assumed that the rank was awarded to the town during the reign of Emperor Caracalla, the son of Septimius Severus, who stayed in the city during his father's military campaigns of AD 208–11.

The Buildings of York's *Colonia*

The south side of the River Ouse remains on a gentle slope and the north side is on a slight plateau overlooking the south bank. The civilian settlement on the south side of the river would have always been on this slope and probably within reach of the flooding Ouse on occasion. The highest geographical point in Roman York, a point given the modern name of 'The Mount', sits a few hundred metres southwards of the city walls and overlooks most of the southern part of the city – it would have been from this direction that foot and vehicle traffic would approach the city, travelling first through a cemetery that stretched outwards up and over this hill before coming into *Eboracum* through a gatehouse near Mickelgate Bar. That road itself may have had shops and housing grow up on it over time.

We are, again, hampered by a lack of large and modern excavations to the level of the Roman remains within the area of the *colonia*, but a few antiquarian excavations have revealed some interesting features about the domestic makeup of the area. We can be reasonable sure that was lot of housing here, and possibly a *Forum* and other municipal places expected of a large town.

Perhaps of most interest is the largest single house we know about here – the so-called 'House of the Three Mosaics' in Toft Green. South of the river and set back from the immediate riverfront and its trade activity and above the flood-line, only a fragment of this huge house has been identified. Three conjoining, roughly square rooms were identified during excavations in 1853, each including a grand floor mosaic in an excellent state of preservation.

One of these, the mosaic depicting the Four Seasons, has been reconstructed and redisplayed on the floor of a gallery in the Yorkshire Museum. The figures on it are Summer with a bunch of grapes (a Victorian edit from the original flower), Spring with a swallow on her shoulder, Autumn with a rake (a local, Romano-British depiction of this season) and Winter with a bare branch.

A complex of particularly high status buildings, including the House of the Three Mosaics, and part of a bathhouse to the north of it have been tentatively suggested as parts of a large residence used by the Governor of northern Britain. Originally *Britannia* was a single province but it was split into two provinces (*Britannia Superior* in the south and *Britannia Inferior* in the north) in the early third century. *Eboracum* became the capital of *Britannia Inferior* and thus the seat of the Governor of the province. A dedication to 'The Gods of the legate's residence', punched into a small bronze tablet

Only the most affluent buildings and households in Roman York would have been decorated with mosaics. They were often inspired by mythological scenes. Toft Green, 1840. In the Yorkshire Museum (YORYM: 1998.24). (©York Museums Trust (Yorkshire Museum) [CC BY-SA 4.0])

in Greek lettering, recovered from the Old Railway Station in 1840 is the best literary evidence we have for a high-status building in the *colonia*. Whoever lived in this house, in the prime real-estate of York, was a wealthy person indeed.

Although less famous within the confines of Roman York, the most familiar building in the *colonia* is probably the bathhouse. While only a fragment of one of the plunge pools has been discovered, beneath the road leading from modern-day Lendal Bridge towards the train station, it was clearly a monumental structure. To appreciate the potential scale of the bathhouse we need only turn to the similarly sized (but more complete) bathhouse at *Ratae Coritanorum* (Leicester) which covered an area of 50 m x 25 m. The surviving

The reconstructed mosaic depicting the four seasons, on display in the Yorkshire Museum. (YORYM: 2002.478) (©York Museums Trust (Yorkshire Museum) [CC BY-SA 4.0])

palaestra wall of this bathhouse, the modern 'Jewry Wall', survives to a height of over 9 m, providing an insight into just how imposing this structure truly was. The bathhouse was a prominent landmark in this part of town.

The discovery of two separate fragments of statuary associated with the Mithraic cult on the south side of the river also offers a strong suggestion that the temple to Mithras must have existed within this area. It not surprising to find a temple to this military-themed religion in a town with such a large military presence, nor one to Mars. A large statue of Mars along with several altars dedicated to the god were found redeposited in a pit at the edge of the settlement and probably all came from a temple nearby.

Fragments of many other stone buildings are known from this area. Suffice to say that the place was busy and crowded and, no doubt, constantly under renovation, demolition and/or expansion.

A copper alloy plaque inscribed in Greek with punched lettering with a dedication to the Gods of the Legate's Praetorium. It was found on the south side of the river in the *colonia*. Old Railway Station, 1840. In the Yorkshire Museum (YORYM: H4.2). (©York Museums Trust (Yorkshire Museum) [CC BY-SA 4.0])

The Jewry Wall museum bathhouse, Leicester, which still stands to an impressive 8 metres in height. (Public Domain (Alex Liivet) via Wikimedia Commons)

Governance

The legionary legate was responsible for the fortress and the soldiers under his command and, to a certain extent, the policing and security of the non-military parts of *Eboracum*. He was not the only figure involved in the running of the city. The inscription on the sarcophagus of Flavius Bellator identifies him as a decurion – a man of civil rank (loosely akin to a local councillor or MP). Early in the Imperial period, aristocratic citizens actively sought the post as a mark of prestige; they would gain civic privileges and be accepted as *honestiores* (honourable men) – useful, perhaps, for tradespeople or the socially mobile. Another decurion, Claudius Florentius, was the dedicator of the tombstone to his father, Antonius Gargilianus. The decurions were always elected from the middle classes – the *eques*, or 'knights' – and were comfortable-living, affluent men. Gargilianus is named as being 'of equestrian rank' on his tomb and this would mean his son, Claudius, was also middle class and thus eligible for the rank he held. Flavius Bellator wore a gold ring set with a ruby when he was buried at the age of twenty-nine; the gold ring was a status symbol of the middle social rank in the Roman Empire and it is certainly of importance that he was buried wearing it.

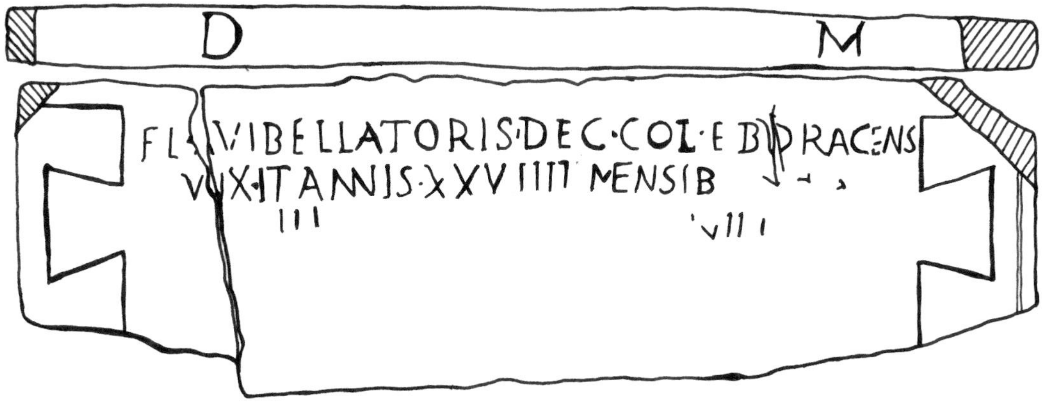

A sarcophagus bearing an inscription naming Flavius Bellator, Decurion of the colony of *Eboracum*. (Redrawn by the author from the original in Collingwood and Wright, 1966, *Roman Inscriptions of Britain*)

Once elected, the decurions were expected to use their own money to invest in public-spirited building projects and even to compete to furnish their communities with the best civic buildings – temples, bathhouses, fountains, art, etc. At the end of the third century, problems with the Empire's finances forced the role of decurion to change to that of tax-collector, who were then expected to make up any shortfall in their local tax collection from their own income. Many decurions illegally left their positions in an attempt to avoid this burden, but faced execution for doing so.

'To the Shades of the Departed'

The rediscovery of buried human remains, along with any associated grave goods, provides archaeologists with an almost unparalleled research resource into aspects of daily life including diet, migration, health, religion and superstition.

At the occasion of a death in the Roman world, in domestic circumstances it very much became a family affair. The body was usually laid out at home, cleaned and perfumed before being taken on a procession from their house to the place of burial or cremation. Military funerals were conducted by the soldiers themselves and were often paid for by the 'burial fund', paid incrementally from a soldier's pay into a central pot for this purpose.

Cemeteries

Roman cemeteries were always outside of the city walls, for reasons of hygiene, and frequently followed the major roads into or out of the city. Every road leaving York has yielded some evidence for a cemetery close by – the city was literally surrounded by them. Cemetery sites are known from the Mount, Fishergate, Driffield Terrace, Trentholme Drive, Lawrence Street and the railway station. The latter was by far the largest. In fact, the railway station and the Mount cemeteries may be a single, elongated necropolis leading from the river on the south-west side of the *colonia* to the highest point in the immediate landscape. Cemeteries catered for all social classes in the Roman world, the only real indicator of status being the nature of the objects placed into the grave with the deceased.

To offer an indication of the size of a Roman cemetery, we need only turn to the first formal excavation of one in Britain – Trentholme Drive, located south-west of the *colonia* on the Mount. Discovered entirely by chance in 1951 by schoolchildren, Trentholme Drive was excavated by Leslie Peter Wenham. The Trentholme Drive excavations were, really, a small spotlight into the much, much larger cemetery site mentioned above. The area, measuring 43 m x 22 m, yielded fifty-three cremations and over 300 burials. Many of the burials cut into earlier ones, showing that the cemetery was used over a long time.

The cemeteries of York were covered with monuments to the departed. Tombstones and grave markers came in all shapes and sizes from small plaques or wooden stakes to huge stone crypts with lockable doors. Many festivals throughout the Roman calendar

Excavated by L. P. Wenham in the 1950s, the cemetery at Trentholme Drive is one of the busiest that we have found. Note the close proximity and differing alignments of the graves and, also, that at least one here has been cut into by a later grave (only the legs of the skeleton survive). (Image from the Yorkshire Museum archive)

Not every Roman grave was marked by a tombstone but a large, professionally carved tombstone was a sign of affluence and status. This carving depicts Candida Barita and her daughter Mantinia Maerica in a traditional dining scene. The Mount, 1922. In the Yorkshire Museum (YORYM: 2007.2902). (©York Museums Trust (Yorkshire Museum) [CC BY-SA 4.0])

honoured the dead and family ancestors, so the graves may have been well looked after. The huge cemeteries would have been another really prominent place in the landscape of *Eboracum*.

The Emperor Septimius Severus died in York in AD 211 and was famously cremated here in a ceremony held to the west of the city. Cremation was the dominant tradition in the first and second centuries AD but became more and more unfashionable throughout Roman Britain during the third and fourth centuries AD. York, however, has some amazing cremation evidence from this period with the use of elaborate 'head pots' in the city. A head pot depicted a realistic-looking human face and used the entire circumference of the pot to give this impression. The imperial family temporarily lived in York between AD 208 and 211. A pair of head pots showing the likeness of the Empress Julia Domna and her son (and later, Emperor) Caracalla have been found and there is nothing else quite like them from anywhere else in Britain. The Julia Domna head pot is from a small cemetery at Fishergate, south-east of the city. She is depicted as a true Roman matron, both poised and elegant. Her hair is in the same style (tied up in bunches and pulled back from the face) that we find on coins that show her face. Caracalla wears a diadem on his pot, identifying him as the Emperor. Both have been used as cremation containers in York. It is likely that both represent examples of celebrity-worship related to the imperial family – commemorative jars depicting the faces of the most powerful people in the known world is an understandable phenomenon.

Head pots depicting the Empress Julia Domna (left) and her son, and later Emperor, Caracalla (right). In the Yorkshire Museum (YORYM: H2132 & H2135). (©York Museums Trust (Yorkshire Museum) [CC BY-SA 4.0])

Inhumation

An inhumation is a burial in which the body is physically placed in a prepared hole in the ground. It might be in a coffin made of wood or lead, or without. This practice rose in popularity in the third century AD and largely replaced cremation as the primary method for funerals in the second half of the Roman period in Britain. This change is particularly clear at York, where long-standing cemeteries gradually changed from one to the other.

Returning for a closer look at the Trentholme Drive cemetery, a huge range of information about the population of Roman York has been gleaned from the excavations here. As mentioned, over 300 individuals were physically buried at this site. The geographical extent of the south-western necropolis of Roman York has not been defined; the total number of buried individuals in this one site must have ran into the thousands by the end of the fourth century, and this was only one of a number of cemeteries serving *Eboracum*. Trentholme Drive included individuals ranging from infants a few months old to adults over the age of sixty. Most were buried without a coffin or container of any kind, but wooden coffins closed with iron nails, lead coffins, stone-lined graves and stone sarcophagi were used in small numbers. The posture of the skeletal remains discovered is often used by archaeologists as indicators of ritual, belief or tradition, but no trends were visible at this particular cemetery, with a range of poses evident. The excavator suggested that the unusual positioning of several skeletons may be evidence of their inhumation after rigor mortis had set in, preventing the movement of limbs. One of the most interesting and unusual burials from this cemetery site was of two men, one in his late teens and one in his early twenties, buried with the older man wrapping his left arm around the younger man and clasping his shoulder in a protective embrace.

Other burials from York reveal different pieces of information about the ancient city. Perhaps the most famous burial dates from the early third century, from Sycamore Terrace, and was of an adult female aged between eighteen and twenty-five. Recent osteological analyses have shown the young lady was of North African descent; a fascinating insight when considered alongside her grave goods. She was buried wearing two pairs of bangles – one in African elephant ivory, the other in Whitby jet – a pair of amber earrings, a blue glass necklace, and with a mirror and a fine glass unguent bottle. The bangles show a fascinating link between international and local fashions and were worn in combination with Baltic amber and German glass – all difficult to come by, high-status objects. Most interesting is the inclusion of a small, openwork plaque carved with a Christian greeting.

York may also have had its own special burial ground for gladiators – the excavations of Driffield Terrace found many skeletons which had been decapitated

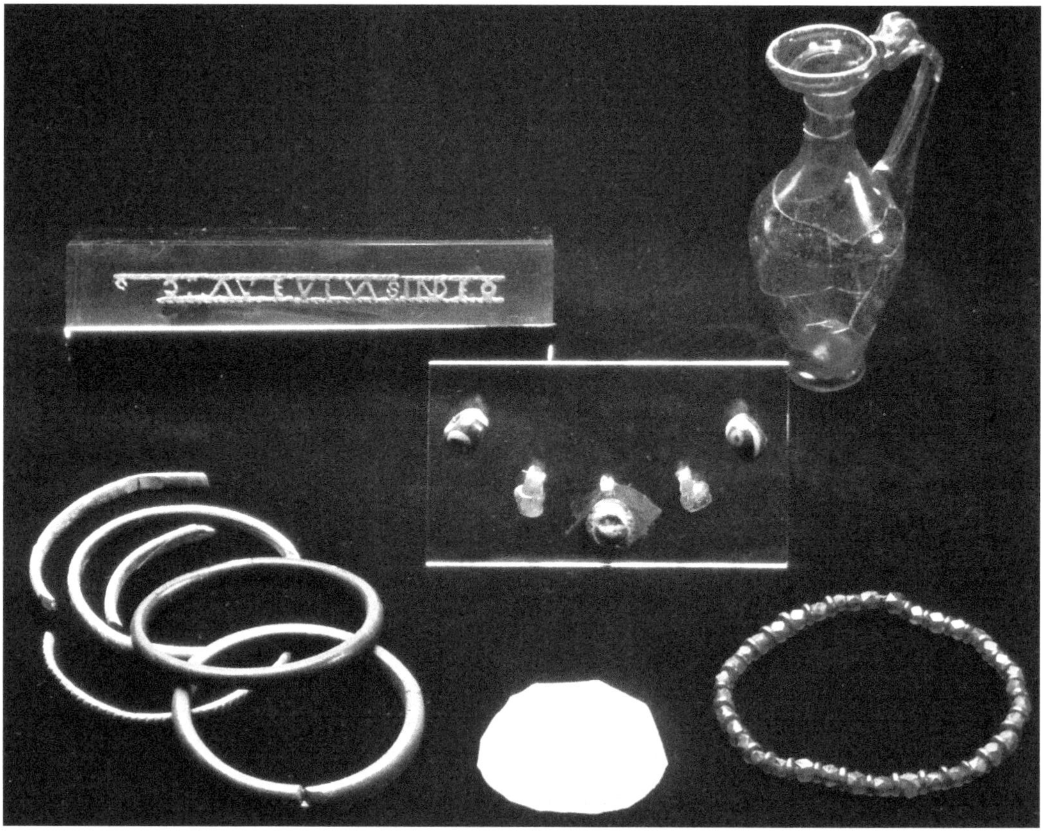

The grave goods of the so-called 'Ivory Bangle Lady'. In the Yorkshire Museum. (©York Museums Trust (Yorkshire Museum) [CC BY SA 4.0])

at the time of their deaths and one which had a bite mark on his pelvis caused by a large animal such as a tiger or a bear.

Some of the best information about the lives of the deceased comes from stone sarcophagi. The sarcophagi in York were all huge sandstone boxes, some of which were inscribed with epitaphs and sculpture on the sides, and all were capped by a large stone slab. The body inside the sarcophagus was placed within a lead coffin and often covered in gypsum. Gypsum acts as kind of mortar, sealing the body into the coffin and often leading to the unusual preservation of skeletal remains part-encased in plaster, mineralised textile fragments from shrouds, and even human hair. Recent chemical analysis of the York gypsum burials has shown that resins such as exotic frankincense (from Ethiopia) may have been added into these burials.

One gypsum burial in York uniquely preserved the auburn hair of a young woman still held up by the jet hairpins used to style it. It is unknown what process has helped

Gypsum was used to cover the bodies, within a coffin, in some late Roman inhumations. You are looking at the underside of this example, but it bears the impressions of two adults, each laying on their sides, facing each other, with a swaddled infant between their legs. Bishopgate/Princes Street, 1851. In the Yorkshire Museum (YORYM: 2007.6126). (©York Museums Trust (Yorkshire Museum) [CC BY SA 4.0])

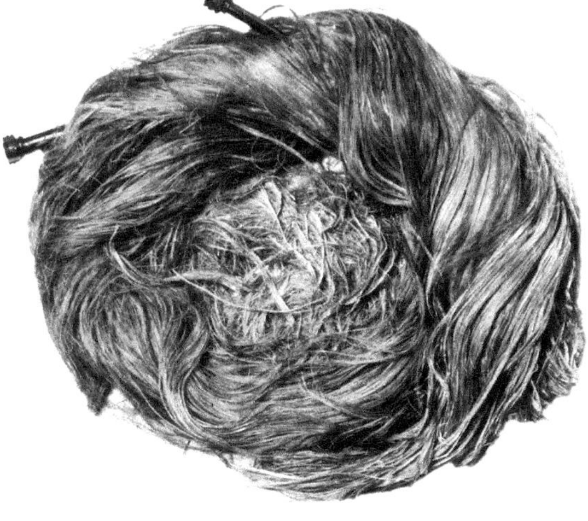

Auburn hair, held up with a pair of jet hairpins, preserved by gypsum in a sarcophagus burial from the railway station. In the Yorkshire Museum (YORYM: 1998.695). (©York Museums Trust (Yorkshire Museum) [CC BY SA 4.0])

this hair fragment survive, but it is presumed that some chemical additive was included into the burial to facilitate this amazing preservation.

Sarcophagi also offer the rather unique opportunity to associate the bodies inside to the name written on the exterior. Recording this information means that the remains of Aurelius Superus, Flavius Bellator and Aelia Severa are known to us by name. Of course, this is not a foolproof method of investigation as the occasional re-use of sarcophagi by different people has been known: the sarcophagus of Julia Fortunata was actually discovered to contain the remains of an old man.

Aurelius Superus was a centurion in the 6th Legion. He died aged thirty-eight and was commemorated in this inscription by his wife. The sarcophagus is shown here on display in the early twentieth century. Castle Yard, 1835. (Image from the Yorkshire Museum archive)

Gods and Magic

Gods, Goddesses, Places

Roman religion, generally, was based around a core of twelve deities known as the Pantheon. They are: Jupiter, Juno, Minerva, Mars, Venus, Apollo, Diana, Ceres, Mercury, Neptune, Vulcan and Vesta – each of which has a long history based in ancient Greek myths. By the time Britain was invaded, Roman religion had become a firmly established phenomenon but it, really very importantly, was not exclusive to just these gods. Everywhere the Roman Empire extended to, and every new population or culture it came into contact with, resulted in the absorption of the new gods into the Roman religion. Where newly encountered gods clearly served a similar purpose to a named Roman god, they are often melded together via a process called 'syncretism' – creating many double-barrelled deities in Roman Britain including Sulis-Minerva and Mars-Thincsus. In other cases, an already 'joined-up' god is brought into the province in its new duplicated manner: Jupiter-Dolichenus is an excellent example of this, having being imported into Britain in the late second or third century by the army.

The worship of the well-established deities of War (Mars), Love (Venus) or the Sea (Neptune) are only part of the story in York. Evidence, in various forms, records the worship of numerous deities from Roman York:

Classical Gods	**Eastern Gods**	**Personifications**	**Local/British**
Hercules	Apis Bull (Osiris)	*Bonus Eventus*	Arciaco
Imperial Cult	Arimanius	*Britannia*	Dioscuri
Jupiter	Atys/Cybele	Fortune	*Genius Locus*
Mars	Chnoubis	Hospitality	*Genii Eboraci*
Mercury	Isis	Ocean	Mother Goddesses
Priapus	Mithras	Victory	Sucellus
Silvanus	Serapis		Toutatis
Tethys			The *Veteres*
Venus			Veteris

Table 1. The gods of *Eboracum* divided by category.

Roman religion was so diverse that there was an assumption built into it that all places had gods associated with them and that these gods can be venerated even without knowing their true names. This is where the *Genius Locus/Genii Loci* come in. *Genius*

An altar dedicated to the *Genii Loci*, the 'Gods of the Place'. Railway station, 1875. In the Yorkshire Museum (YORYM: 2007.6199). (©York Museums Trust (Yorkshire Museum) [CC BY SA 4.0])

refers to the essence or soul, and *Locus* to 'the place' or 'this place'. 'The Gods of the Place', as they are commonly referred to, were an important element in Roman religion across the Empire and are attested at York. Most interestingly, a fragmentary inscription found beneath the railway station in 1909 offers a dedication to 'The Imperial Name and the *Genius Eboraci*' or, more specifically, to the 'Gods of *Eboracum*'.

The best literary evidence for religion comes from the names inscribed on altar stones. An altar was a stone pillar, taller than it is wide, on which an abbreviated Latin inscription was carved on the front face. Altars were set up at religious and spiritual sites, as well as private houses and roadsides. A telling phrase on the base of many of these shows how Roman religion functioned on a day-to-day basis – the phrase VSLM is an abbreviation of VOTUM SOLVIT LIBENS MERITO, literally 'a vow willingly and deservedly fulfilled'. This shows us that the altar has been dedicated as payment for divine favour. The nature of the request is rarely ever recorded on the stone as most altars act as a sort of receipt for a private bargain between an individual and a god for services rendered. The service might be hunting success, a safe voyage, a good harvest, gambling victories, a safe childbirth, or any one of hundreds of unknowable needs and wants. At least twenty-three individual Latin inscriptions from York highlight this bargained relationship between the people and their gods. A rare example of an altar which reveals what vow was actually being fulfilled wasn't found in York, but does records the exploits of someone who worked here:

> DEAE TVELE BOVDIG
> M AVR LVNARIS SE
> VIR AVG COL EBOR ET
> LIND PROV BRIT INF
> ARAM QVAM VOVER
> AB EBORACI EVECT
> V S L M
> PERPETVO TE CORNE

The text reads:

> To the guardian goddess Boudiga, Marcus Aurelius Lunaris, *servir Augustalis* of the colonies of *Eboracum* and *Lindum* in the province of *Britannia Inferior*, promised solemnly this altar on sailing from *Eboracum*. He willingly and deservedly fulfilled his vow in the consulship of Perpetuus and Cornelianus.

Altar dedicated at Bordeaux by a priest of York and Lincoln, Marcus Aurelius Lunaris. Bordeaux, 1921.

Marcus was a priest of the Imperial Cult, responsible for the colonies at both *Eboracum* (York) and *Lindum* (Lincoln) who asked for safe passage across the North Sea from a goddess named Boudiga, and who fulfilled his part of the 'divine bargain' upon arrival in Bordeaux – where this altar was located. The names of the two Roman officials at the end allow us to date this stone quite precisely to AD 237. Quite interestingly, the stone used is a type of millstone grit quarried from Yorkshire and was, presumably, carried across the sea for this specific purpose. We know of at least one other priest from York – Marcus Verecundius Diogenes, a native Gaul, who died while serving as a priest in York.

Many of the gods of York are known to us only by name. Arciaco and Dioscuri are two such examples. The same goes for Toutatis. 'Toutatis', or 'Totatis', most famously used as a war-cry by the fictional, feisty Gaul Asterix ('By Toutatis!'), is a god recorded from the north-western Roman provinces. He is most commonly recorded from silver rings which bear an abbreviation of his name (TOT) and it is through the discovery of one such example at York that we have Toutatis attested here.

Where the images of gods survive, they are often shown in a very similar format throughout the Roman Empire, with specific poses, objects, totems or avatars used repeatedly as ways to present them to the public. Thus the statue of Mars from Mickelgate is shown as a young man dressed like a soldier – wearing a breastplate and a helmet, carrying a shield in his left hand. His right hand is missing, but it would have originally held a spear, like on a red jasper intaglio (a semi-precious gemstone setting from a finger-ring) from the Church Street sewer. Venus appears naked on small ceramic statues, mass-produced in central Gaul in the first three centuries AD, in which she is shown as a curvaceous, long-haired lady with one hand in her hair and one on her hips; appropriate imagery for the Goddess of Love.

Silver ring bearing the inscription TOT, an abbreviation of Toutatis. TOT rings are the most common form of dedication to this Gallic god. In the Yorkshire Museum (YORYM: 2001.12509). (©York Museums Trust (Yorkshire Museum) [CC BY SA 4.0])

She is particularly important as a symbol of fertility and protection, and the use of Venus figurines in graves has been interpreted as connected with women who died in childbirth. We also see deities depicted in miniature statues of copper-alloy and decorated on mosaic floors.

Eastern religions and mysticism were a constant source of interest in the Roman period. The cult of Isis is thought to have been brought to York in the early third century

A fourth-century statue of Mars, the god of war. Bar Convent, Nunnery Lane, 1880. In the Yorkshire Museum (YORYM: 1998.26). (©York Museums Trust (Yorkshire Museum) [CC BY SA 4.0])

Mars depicted on a red jasper intaglio (ring setting). Church Street, 1972. In the Yorkshire Museum (YORYM: 19672.22.6020). (©York Museums Trust (Yorkshire Museum) [CC BY SA 4.0])

A ceramic figurine depicting the goddess Venus (the fine ceramic is often referred to as 'pipe-clay'). Tanner Row, York, 1983. In the Yorkshire Museum (YORYM: 1983.32.2275). (©York Museums Trust (Yorkshire Museum) [CC BY SA 4.0])

by the visiting Severan Imperial family. Perhaps the most famous of the 'Eastern gods' is Mithras. His cult, Mithraism, can be found anywhere in the Roman Empire where a strong military presence was felt and the army was probably instrumental in spreading it. The imagery of the cult is quite unique – the primary iconography is the 'Tauroctony' or 'killing of the bull'. Mithras is depicted as a strong man, wearing a Phrygian cap (denoting his 'Eastern' origins) and his cape blows heroically behind him. His left knee rests upon a giant bull, pinning it to the floor, while he holds its head back with one hand and plunges a dagger into its neck with the other. The life-blood of the bull attracts the attention of a small dog, a scorpion, a snake and a raven. He is usually joined by his

The Tauroctony Scene, an integral image of the worship of Mithras, from Toft Green, York. In the Yorkshire Museum (YORYM: 2007.6125). (©York Museums Trust (Yorkshire Museum) [CC BY SA 4.0])

two companions, Cautes and Cautopates, the twin torch-bearers – one of whom raises his torch to the sky and the other to the floor. Although it has been heavily weathered over time this Tauroctony altar from the York *colonia* would have originally resided in a small rectangular temple, of which no trace has survived.

Temples

Unhelpfully, there is no structural evidence that survives of the many temples which must have existed in York throughout the Roman period. Not every god had, or needed, a temple to be worshipped from, but they were used. We wouldn't expect to find a grand 'classical temple' with a huge colonnade here as few such temples are known from Britain (Bath, Colchester and Maryport). By far the most common temple format is the 'Romano-British' temple, comprising a small, square tower surrounded by a walkway.

Claudius Hieronymanius, Legate of the 6th Legion at the end of the second century AD, constructed a temple to the god Serapis in the area of Tanner Row, immediately south of the River Ouse, and recorded this achievement in writing. A fragmentary inscription from Nessgate, dedicated to Hercules, recorded the reconstruction of a structure – presumably a temple given the inclusion of the god's name on it. A third, and final, inscription mentioning a temple again recorded its reconstruction – probably dedicated to the Imperial Cult.

A typical example of a Romano-British temple, showing the floorplan of the central tower. Like the other temples in York, this example was situated in a prominent place in the landscape. Jordan's Hill, Dorset. (©August Schwerdfeger via Wikimedia Commons [CC BY-Attribution 4.0])

Dedication stone recording the rebuilding of a temple to Hercules. In the Yorkshire Museum (YORYM: 2007.6186). (©York Museums Trust (Yorkshire Museum) [CC BY SA 4.0])

Early Christianity

Constantine the Great, proclaimed as Emperor in York in AD 306, is famous for being the first Roman Emperor to stop persecutions against the Christian communities of the Roman period. The Edict of Milan (AD 313) legalised Christianity and returned confiscated property back to the Church. Constantine was brought up under the influence of his mother, Helen, a devout Christian, but it wasn't until he was in his early forties that he formally converted to Christianity. This influence is celebrated in the canonisation of his mother as St Helena of Constantinople by the Catholic Church in later years.

One of the few definitively Christian objects from Roman York is an ivory plaque, carved into the phrase SOROR AVE VIVAS IN DEO, 'Hail Sister, may you live in God!'

This plaque was one of several objects placed in a female burial dating from the late third or early fourth century AD. She is known colloquially as the 'Ivory Bangle Lady' – a name given by the discovery of elephant ivory bangles upon her wrists. While it is an

The ivory plaque bearing a Christian inscription, buried with the 'Ivory Bangle Lady'. In the Yorkshire Museum. (©York Museums Trust (Yorkshire Museum) [CC BY SA 4.0])

excellent indication of the existence of a member of the early Christian community at *Eboracum*, this plaque does not definitively prove that the woman with whom it was interred was also Christian. The north–south alignment of the burial and the inclusion of other objects in the grave is more suggestive of a pagan burial into which a Christian object has been placed by someone for whom it held more religious significance.

Few other artefacts survive from York's early Christian communities, but there is evidence enough to know that it was being practiced here in the Roman period. A stone discovered at excavations beneath York Minster (in the area beneath the headquarters building of the fortress) was marked with a Chi-Rho symbol carved upon it. Early Christian symbology frequently used these two letters to signify the first letter-sounds of 'Christ'. Fish were also commonly used as Christian symbols during the Roman period (based on the use of the Greek name for fish, *ichthys*, as a mnemonic for the Latin phrase 'Jesus Christ, son of God, Saviour'; an intaglio (ring setting) excavated from Wellington Row depicts two fish hanging from an anchor.

Magic

Objects included under the umbrella of 'magic' include amulets, charms, curses and some protective images and gestures. For example, a gold charm written in Greek was designed to protect its wearer from stomach complaints by invoking the Gnostic deity Chnoubis. It was written on a thin sheet of gold foil only a few centimetres wide, and originally rolled up and worn in a small amulet case or tube. The amulet was believed to work through a combination of the arcane and unusual words, written on the right material, being worn in a certain way.

Three phallic carvings were uncovered in excavations on the fortress wall and were designed to deflect the gaze of the evil eye. Known as the *malus oculus* in Latin, the eye was the Roman personification of bad luck and was both feared and respected throughout the period. Phallic imagery was regarded as one of its enemies and functioned like a lightning conductor for bad luck. The phallic image is often shown physically attacking an eye in carvings elsewhere in Roman Britain. In York it also occurs on small metal objects of personal adornment, most commonly associated with soldiers. Sometimes these join one magical image with another – in the case of the 'fist-and-phallus' pendants, it is the phallus with a hand making a good-luck gesture. This gesture, the *manus fica* ('fig sign'), was the Roman equivalent of crossing your fingers for luck.

One of three phallic carvings found near the west wall of the fortress, designed to defend the wall or the inhabitants of the fortress from supernatural harm. In the Yorkshire Museum (YORYM: 2007.6142). (©York Museums Trust (Yorkshire Museum) [CC BY SA 4.0])

Three jet pendants each depicting a Medusa head have been found in York. These are part of a small but now well defined group of *gorgoneia* pendants in Roman jet, of which a total of only eleven are recorded from Britain. The evidence points towards all being worn by young adult women, as they appear in rich graves which often include other jet objects. Two of three York *gorgoneia* have been worn smooth on the face, suggesting that they had been rubbed between fingers over a long period of time. Jet was electrostatic and rubbing it in this way may have had a very real physical effect (such as attracting hair or cloth fibres) that would have fascinated the minds of the Roman women using them and, perhaps more importantly, reinforced its use as a 'magical' object.

Second-century BC mosaic from the 'House of the Evil Eye', in Antioch, depicting the evil eye surrounded by its enemies. (©Public Domain via Wikimedia Commons)

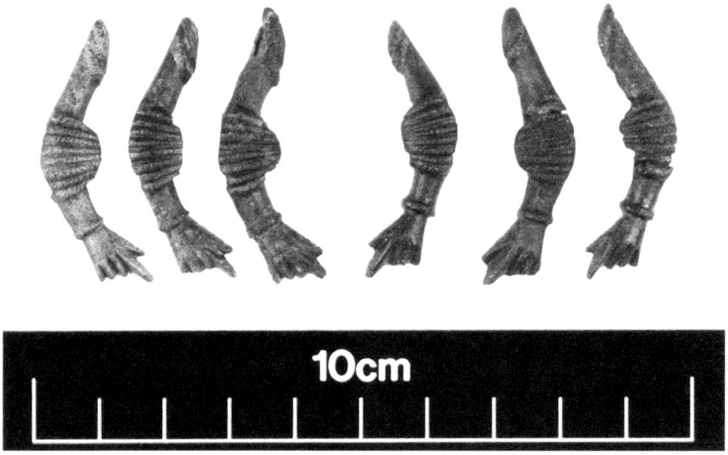

A unique group of fist-and-phallus pendants from an infant grave at Catterick, North Yorkshire. In the Yorkshire Museum (YORYM: 1980.54.9464.1-6). (©York Museums Trust (Yorkshire Museum) [CC BY SA 4.0])

Jet *gorgoneia* from York. In the Yorkshire Museum (YORYM: H320.1, H321.14, H2443).

Dress and Dining

Eboracum, although at the very limit of the Roman Empire geographically, was still party to ever-changing trends. Just like today, clothing, jewellery and hairstyle could be used to indicate different things: religion, economic status, seasonal practicality, social mobility, military or political rank, nationality, age and simple vanity. The type and range of foods available were also fashionable and often linked to changes in the wider Empire. Roman fashions were fickle, changing quickly between generations. There is nothing to suggest that the provincial town of York was in any way behind the fashions of the rest of the Empire, or Rome itself. As well as the international styles which are prevalent throughout the Roman period, local, regional or provincial fashions can be discovered within the archaeological record.

Dress

There are no convenient, well-dated suits of Roman clothes that have survived to the modern day which allow us to show all the changes over the period. Some basic items of clothing remain quite familiar throughout the period – leather shoes, usually with iron hobnailed soles, for example, were the standard footwear used to plod the streets of York. Equally, the woollen tunic remained a staple element of clothing throughout. Silks were certainly imported from the Far East into the Roman Empire and gold-woven textiles were available to those with the coin to pay for them.

Earrings were predominantly a feminine item of jewellery and usually based on a copper, silver or gold wire thread. They were usually coiled in, or loosely hanging through, the ear and may be plain metal hoops or incorporate semi-precious stones or decorative gold-working elements dangling beneath. A plain gold finger ring on the hand of a man denoted his membership of the middle class, which came with a strictly censored financial qualification incorporating cash and assets. The upper ranks had access to the finest textiles, precious metals and jewels from around the known world. It is difficult to generalise for the whole Roman period, but there are points we pick up. Namely, we often think about Roman citizens wearing togas, the large white cloth wraps which were the 'black tie' outfit of the Roman world, and this would have been the case in *Eboracum* but, importantly, the toga was a ceremonial dress rather than everyday wear. The same is true of the female equivalent, the stola. Tunics and cloaks were much more common as formal outfits.

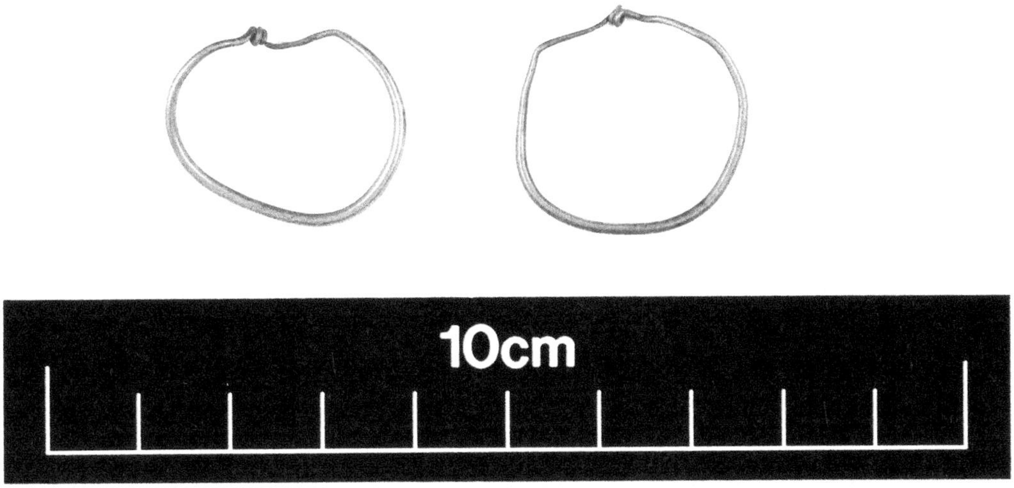

Above: Gold earrings, worn by a young woman in her grave. Heslington, 1831. In the Yorkshire Museum (YORYM: H323.6). (©York Museums Trust (Yorkshire Museum) [CC BY SA 4.0])

Right: Tombstone dedicated by a veteran of the 6th Legion to his wife, Flavia Augustina, and their two children. Note the formal use of tunics and cloaks rather than a toga. In the Yorkshire Museum (YORYM: 1998.18). (©York Museums Trust (Yorkshire Museum) [CC BY SA 4.0])

Probably the most recognisable professional dress in York was the soldiers' – on duty, soldiers wore full body armour and were equipped with sword and shield at all times. They were supposed to be conspicuous. We have found fragments of armour and military decorations from York which themselves show some of the changes in the standard kit worn by the legionaries over three centuries. Some objects would also be visual cues of rank; the vine-stick, for instance, was held by a centurion and used for discipline.

Off-duty soldiers would still have been obvious, even in their 'civilian' dress. Soldiers worn a tunic and a kind of military cloak, often with a military-style belt around the middle – the tombstone of Lucius Duccius Rufinus showed the standard-bearer in his off-duty clothing and this outfit would have been a clear visual cue to the inhabitants of York about the job of the man wearing it.

Detail of a soldier's off-duty clothing, from the tombstone of Lucius Duccius Rufinus, standard-bearer of the 9th Legion. In the Yorkshire Museum (YORYM: 1998.19). (©York Museums Trust (Yorkshire Museum) [CC BY-SA 4.0])

Changing fashions also altered the way people presented themselves and these cues often came from the Imperial family as the major trend-setters of the Roman period. For instance, beards became more popular after the Emperor Hadrian starting sporting one in the early second century AD and never really went out of fashion until Constantine I started a new trend for being clean-shaven in the early fourth century. The same was true of women's hairstyles – styles worn by empresses often became fashionable over time. We have already noted the hair tied in a bun from the grave in York and its link to the style worn by Julia Domna. Tombstones like Rufinus' are useful to show how people wanted to be remembered – the tombstone of Julia Velva shows her in a dynamic social scene, reclining on a dining couch and flanked by her family.

Greater changes are visible in the small objects worn by people. Brooches, for example, were subjected to huge changes through the Roman period in Britain and local or regional trends occasionally sprang up. In the same way that older fashions

Tombstone of Julia Velva, showing the Roman matron reclining on a dining couch and attended by family and servants. In the Yorkshire Museum (YORYM: 1998.25). (©York Museums Trust (Yorkshire Museum) [CC BY SA 4.0])

may be obvious to us today, these objects would have provided the same social cues. Often these trends can be seen over several provinces, but a type of copper-alloy bracelet called a 'cog-wheel bracelet' was unique to Britain and was produced in the mid-third to fourth centuries AD.

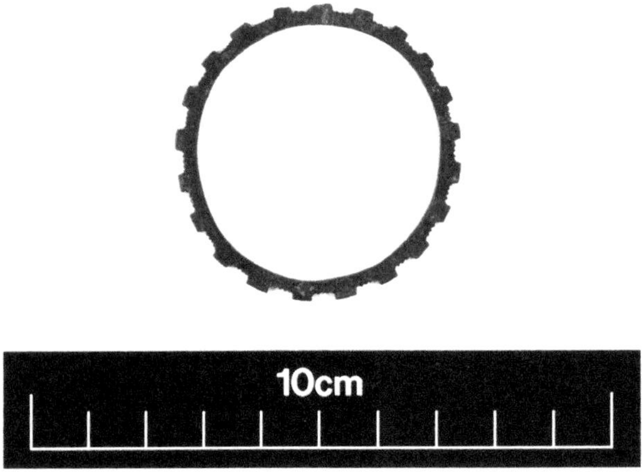

Above: A copper-alloy fantail brooch, with enamel decoration. It dates from the period AD 50–150. Habton, North Yorkshire. PAS: DUR-81CD56. (©Portable Antiquities Scheme [CC BY-Attribution 4.0])

Left: A Romano-British cog-wheel bracelet from an inhumation burial. Heslington, 1831. In the Yorkshire Museum (YORYM: H323.9). (©York Museums Trust (Yorkshire Museum) [CC BY SA 4.0])

It was excavated in Catterick (North Yorkshire), rather than York, but one really special grave in the region gives us an incredible insight into the importance of appearances. The grave was of a young man, but he was buried wearing a large selection of distinctly female jewellery. Archaeologists have excavated thousands of Roman graves in Britain so we have a good idea of what they normally contained and this grave was archaeologically unusual. The explanation for this is that the man was probably a *Gallus* – a priest of the Goddess Cybele who lived as a transvestite, adopting female clothing and jewellery as part of his role in society. The *Galli* ritually castrated themselves as part of their devotion to Cybele – it is really important to show that the simple male/female narrative we can find in archaeology was often more complicated than it first seems.

Dining

The character and content of the dining table in Roman York would not be so dissimilar to anywhere else in Roman Britain because the availability of food stuffs was dependent on local production (and thus affected by seasonality and harvest quality) or national or international importation. The single major factor affecting what food and drink was available was, of course, money. Rare or exotic imported goods would come with an increased price tag.

Eboracum was a large settlement with both military and civilian components existing in a mutually beneficial arrangement. As such, the site had access to great quantities of cattle and pigs, domestic fowl, fish and shellfish, in addition to imported wine, oil and fish sauces. Archaeology has shown that beef was the most commonly butchered meat on site, but that pork featured strongly, along with sheep, goat and even horse. Extensive scientific analysis of Roman environmental deposits has shown that a wide variety of plants were consumed in the city. Oats, spelt wheat and barley were certainly cultivated in the area and were used for bread and brewing. Olives, lentils, grapes, mulberries and figs have all been found in York and were all imported from the continent. A bewildering range of food animals have been identified from the *colonia*. The familiar domestic fowl (chicken) and domestic duck, cattle, sheep/goats feature prominently, but edible crab, oyster, mussels and dormice have also been found. The fish eaten in Roman York include trout, grayling, chub, perch, pike, roach, herring and eel, with the addition of cod and whiting in later periods. A Romano-British diet was, potentially, a varied one, provided for by a heady mix of domestic and home-grown crops and animals added to by exotic, international materials on occasion. We don't have a great understanding of the extent of the farmland surrounding York other than to say just that – York was probably surrounded by them, in addition to large wooded areas, and the landscapes between the large settlements were peppered with field-systems. Both rivers in York would have been fished and access from the Ouse to the coast provided the opportunity for off-shore fish, like herring and cod, to be brought into York.

A staple part of the Roman diet was a rather unusual sauce. Known as *garum* or *muria*, this pickled fish sauce was used as a component and base in a great deal of Roman cookery. 'For soft-boiled eggs: pepper, soaked pine nuts. Add honey and vinegar and mix with garum.' (Columella, *Apicius*, 329)

It was produced in, unsurprisingly, coastal regions of the Mediterranean and transported throughout the Empire. Several qualities and, indeed, prices of the fish sauce existed but the quantity of amphorae bearing this product around the Roman Empire indicates its importance to the ancient culinary tradition. *Garum* was as typically Roman as a Sunday roast is British or pasta is Italian.

Ceramic and metal vessels were used in the Romano-British kitchen and a complicated range of buckets, basins, platters, dippers, strainers, saucepans, skillets, cups, jugs and bowls would make up a standard kitchen assemblage – it is difficult to judge if any, some or all these objects had a long life span. We, perhaps, misjudge the dominance of ceramic materials over metal in the kitchen as the metal materials are frequently melted down and recycled. Occasionally these ceramic jars took on a second life as a cinerary urn for a cremation.

Naturally, the scale of the dining depended upon who, where and when, but lavish tables filled with a feast were reserved, as ever, for the upper classes. Small domestic kitchens of course existed, but if the evidence from historical sources is anything to go by, there would be a wide variety of food stalls and *cauponae* (bars/inns) in the city ready to serve the hungry masses. Snacks could also be purchased in the bathhouses while taking a steam bath. Soldiers were responsible for cooking their own dinner; there was no mess-room to cater for them.

Above left: This grey-ware ceramic jar, inscribed with the details of its original, mundane contents, was re-used as a cremation container. The Mount. In the Yorkshire Museum (YORYM: H142). (©York Museums Trust (Yorkshire Museum) [CC BY SA 4.0])

Above right: A so-called 'cheese press': a perforated ceramic bowl used to drain the whey from curds during cheese-making. In the Yorkshire Museum (YORYM: H2316). (©York Museums Trust (Yorkshire Museum) [CC BY SA 4.0])

Gold, silver or pewter tableware would adorn the tables of the upper echelons – in York we can certainly count the legionary legate and his family among the richest inhabitants of the city; they themselves would pale in comparison to the ostentatious displays of the Imperial family during their short-lived tenures in York. Samian ware is a hugely visible Roman component in the makeup of Romano-British society: it is a hard-wearing, red, glossy ceramic which comes with a staggering range of decorations to choose from. It is largely imported from sites in central and southern Gaul, primarily in the first and second centuries AD. York, like most large settlements in Britain, has its own unique types of ceramic made from local clays – the so-called *Ebor* wares. These are functional, coarse ceramics (most often seen as flagons or bowls) in a sandy-orange colour designed for sale to the local market.

Bronze cauldrons, like this one, are often referred to as 'camp kettles' as they may have been used by soldiers to cook meals together. In the Yorkshire Museum (YORYM: H143). (©York Museums Trust (Yorkshire Museum) [CC BY SA 4.0])

Samian ware, the bright red pottery found all over Roman Britain, was very common in Roman York. It was often decorated with mythological or social scenes. This unusual example is decorated with a group of slaves. In the Yorkshire Museum (YORYM: H32). (©York Museums Trust (Yorkshire Museum) [CC BY SA 4.0])

Industries

The transport and production facilities within *Eboracum* were, of course, key aspects of its domestic, industrial, commercial and military life. The site was part of a much larger and hugely complex network of road, river, and sea transport providing access from this northern outpost to the other end of the Empire.

Roads

The fortress and *colonia* site should be viewed as something of a nexus for the road systems that arrive at or depart from the town. Any map of the Roman town will be seemingly full of straight road lines. In his recent *Secret History of the Roman Roads*

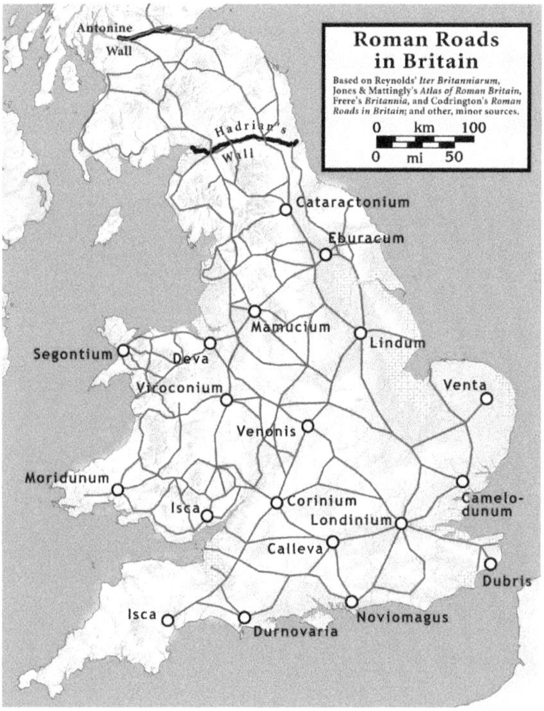

A map of the major road network of Roman Britain. (©Wikimedia Commons [Attribution-SA 3.0])

in Britain, M. C. Bishop sums up the major problem when approaching Roman roads: 'The problems inherent in studying the road system can be summed up eloquently in one simple question: which road system?' All maps of a Roman site should be viewed with a wary eye representing, as they do, only a snap-shot of the area under investigation. Such is the case with York. Like with the changing fortress and the redeveloping town, roads were regularly relayed, moved, widened or built on top of.

A Roman road was rarely paved or flagged outside of a town. They were usually, in Britain, made up of a drainage layer of rubble or boulders topped with compacted sand and gravel ('metalling'). Such roads were built, initially, by the army, then maintained by local towns and cities and used by everyone. Roads were built on a slight camber to help water drain off them and would have been the best option for overland transportation. Wheeled transportation was the only viable option for moving bulk loads of goods around and between towns; the roads surrounding York would have been busy with commercial and pedestrian traffic.

Rivers and the Sea

York is centred on a spit of land at the convergence of the rivers Ouse and Foss. The Ouse's tributaries stem from the North Yorkshire Moors and Yorkshire Dales and its modern incarnation is wide and flat. The Ouse is still navigable and is accessible from the North Sea via the estuary at Hull. The second river here is the Foss, a much narrower river which joins to the Ouse immediately south-east of the ancient city. While modern canalisation of the Foss limits flooding, the two rivers encountered by the inhabitants of Roman York would both have been extremely liable to flooding in the winter months.

It is clear that transport of both products and people was a regular and important element in *Eboracum*'s day-to-day life. A great amount of imported goods would be shipped to the city daily – in many cases the only means of getting goods would be by sea. For example, York was the most northerly settlement in Britain to import a type of amphora only produced in North Africa. Equally, Baltic amber, African ivories and

An international import: earrings made from Baltic amber. Part of the grave assemblage of the 'Ivory Bangle Lady'. In the Yorkshire Museum (YORYM: H8). (©York Museums Trust (Yorkshire Museum) [CC BY SA 4.0])

Spanish oil would have all arrived by sea. The best evidence for an intrepid traveller having left for overseas from the region is the priest who 'set sail from *Eboracum*' on his voyage across the Channel and set up an altar to the Goddess Boudiga in thanks for a safe passage.

Riverine transportation is well documented in Roman Britain, allowing the sailing, rowing or towing of a variety of boats to access *Eboracum*. While no Roman wrecks are available for study at York, the existence of several wharves on the east bank of the Foss identifies a significant level of infrastructure to support river transport. Modern excavations beneath Coney Street identified a huge grain deposit within a large timber structure – a storehouse adjacent to the river and potentially accessible from it. Having so much grain in one place was obviously a problem, as the whole building was burnt down with the grain inside – analyses later found an infestation of grain weevils burnt along with the warehouse, suggesting that it was burnt deliberately to protect the rest of the food supply in *Eboracum*.

Quarried Stone

There was no source of suitable building stone in York within a 15 km radius of the city, but two main types of stone were used in Roman York. The pale yellow-white stone visible in the Multangular Tower and the tombstone of Lucius Duccius Rufinus is the typical limestone used throughout the city. Geologically it is a 'Magnesian Limestone',

Locally quarried magnesian limestone is a pale, white stone which could be easily carved and painted. This altar is dedicated to the mother goddesses by Gaius Julius Crescens. Bar Convent, Nunnery Lane, 1880. In the Yorkshire Museum (YORYM: 2001.12520). (©York Museums Trust (Yorkshire Museum) [CC BY SA 4.0])

A marble statue of an athletic youth. In the Yorkshire Museum (YORYM: 1998.22). (©York Museums Trust (Yorkshire Museum) [CC BY SA 4.0])

but archaeologically it has been transported here from west and south of York. The Roman settlement at modern-day Tadcaster was a probable major source; the Latin name of that town, *Calcaria*, is taken from its connection to the stone. The other major building stone used in York is sandstone – rough, heavy and difficult to carve. The statue of Mars and nearly all of the sarcophagi from the *colonia* cemeteries are made from this sandstone. Both types of stone are heavily affected by weathering. Left exposed to the elements, limestone carvings have been particularly damaged by acid rain during the Industrial Revolution.

While Roman marble statues fill up the galleries of many museums, they really were very rare in provincial Romano-British towns like *Eboracum*. By far the most famous here is the twice life-sized head of the Emperor Constantine from Stonegate. A much smaller marble statue of a youthful athlete is also known from York. Both are probably Carrara marble from the Apennine area of Italy. The nearest Roman *colonia* to York, at *Lindum* (Lincoln), had no recorded marble statues at all until 2014, when the discovery of fragments of a marble bull added another rare example to the small total known from Roman Britain.

Ceramics

The establishment of *Eboracum* brought new trends and innovations in ceramic production to the region – the most obvious is the size of the industry. Roman garrisons needed pottery on a massive scale; over 5,000 soldiers each required access to flagons, cups, plates, dishes, etc. on a day-to-day basis. The rubbish pits throughout York are crammed full of broken pots. The invading army brought new technologies with it in the form of rectangular pottery kilns: 3-metre-wide square boxes with a permanent raised oven-floor on which unfired ('green') pots were placed. A fire was kept in the channel leading to the front, and the fumes leave via a central chimney. Such kilns were easily capable of temperatures between 500°C and 700°C. An area beneath the Borthwick Institute, south-east of the *colonia*, has been suggested as an area used for the production of tiles, but the earliest evidence for production of ceramic vessels at York comes from Aldwalk, between the eastern fortress wall and the River Foss. This area would be ideal for pottery production, given access to the clay in the river for raw materials and the woodland surrounding it for fuel. Evidence for pottery production here starts in AD 71, within weeks or months of the fortress being marked out. In addition to the imported 'fine-wares' from the continent, most forts in the north took responsibility for their own production of day-to-day materials.

As with other places, York has its own unique type of ceramic, the uniqueness coming from the specific mineral content of the local clay used, the temperature and size of the kiln, and the forms preferred by the potters. The so-called *Ebor* ware is biscuit-orange in colour and was most often used for bowls and flagons – the orange colour tells us that there was oxygen flowing throughout the kiln during the entire firing process. It was first produced around AD 71, but a change in the shapes of the rims and the addition of platters and differently shaped bowls from AD 100 might be an indication that the first generation of potters had died or retired and a trend towards development had been taken up by a second generation, or by new migrants to the city.

The use and development of the pottery industry in Britain was, like any industry now, subject to considerable change over time depending on economic, geographical or political factors. The initial mass-importation of ceramics into the province eventually paled in *Britannia* in the face of rising regional and local industry. Ceramic industries became so locally specialised that the character of ancient pottery finds between sites that are geographically close can be quite different – like between York and Doncaster, for example. The third and fourth centuries of Roman York saw local importation of pottery from sites at Holme-on-Spalding Moor, Rossington Bridge, Cantley and Crambeck to name but a few. All of these are quite unique in the range of vessel forms, colours, patterns, as well as the look and type of the clays used. From further south in Britain, York gets black-burnished ware from Dorset, colour-coated ware from the Nene Valley/Peterborough area and others from Oxford and London. And that is just a few of those from Britain; international imports come from central and southern Gaul, Trier (Germany), North Africa and Spain.

The Crambeck ware industry, in particular, is of interest to the later history of Roman York as it developed a rather beautiful series of red-painted wares at a time when many

Above left: The local stuff – an orange-coloured *Ebor* ware ceramic jar. Bar Convent, Nunnery Lane, 1871. In the Yorkshire Museum (YORYM: H2255). (©York Museums Trust (Yorkshire Museum) [CC BY SA 4.0])

Above right: Glossy, black pottery with white decoration like this was all produced in Trier and imported from the late second to third century AD. The text reads VIVATIS ('Long life to you') and may have been a sort of toast. In the Yorkshire Museum (YORYM: H154). (©York Museums Trust (Yorkshire Museum) [CC BY SA 4.0])

Late Roman pottery from Crambeck, North Yorkshire. The ware often features red lines painted over the cream-coloured base fabric. In the Yorkshire Museum (YORYM: H2275). (©York Museums Trust (Yorkshire Museum) [CC BY SA 4.0])

other regional ceramic industries were in decline. Based at Crambeck, near Malton, North Yorkshire, and north-east from York, the Crambeck ware industry blossomed in the fourth century, with its main consumer very clearly York. The interesting designs included stripes, triangles, polka-dots and human figures. Very little of it can be found south of the River Humber, but it did spread over most of North and East Yorkshire, Cumbria, County Durham and Northumberland.

Metalworking

Structural and small finds debris suggest the presence of a blacksmith within the fortress itself. The tombstone of an unnamed blacksmith was discovered in Dringhouses, well outside of the fortress, and shows a heavily bearded man at work on his anvil, hammer held raised in his right hand and tongs in his left. The blacksmith was, in this instance, defined and commemorated by his job – throughout history considered an important one.

Tombstone of a blacksmith. In the Yorkshire Museum (YORYM: 1998.20). (©York Museums Trust (Yorkshire Museum) [CC BY SA 4.0])

Objects made from the many alloys of copper and tin generally survive in the archaeological record a lot better than iron. Copper alloys were used to create a mind-boggling range of objects from bracelets and finger-rings through bowls and flagons, plaques, furniture and chariot wheels to statues both monumental and miniature. Metal objects were frequently recycled in the Roman world, leading to the preservation of much fewer than were in general circulation. Copper alloys were predominantly copper (*c.* 70–80 per cent) with the rest made up by tin (to make bronze), brass, lead and zinc. The science of metallurgy was clearly well understood in the Roman period – statues have a higher lead content to improve their cast strength, mirrors a higher tin content to produce a greater shine, and the specific contents of the alloys suggests that recipes were being used in their production. Most objects conform to the same metal compositions all across the Empire, suggesting they are being traded over large distances. Two types of brooches – the dragonesque and fantail brooches – have been suggested to have been produced and used primarily in Yorkshire and the

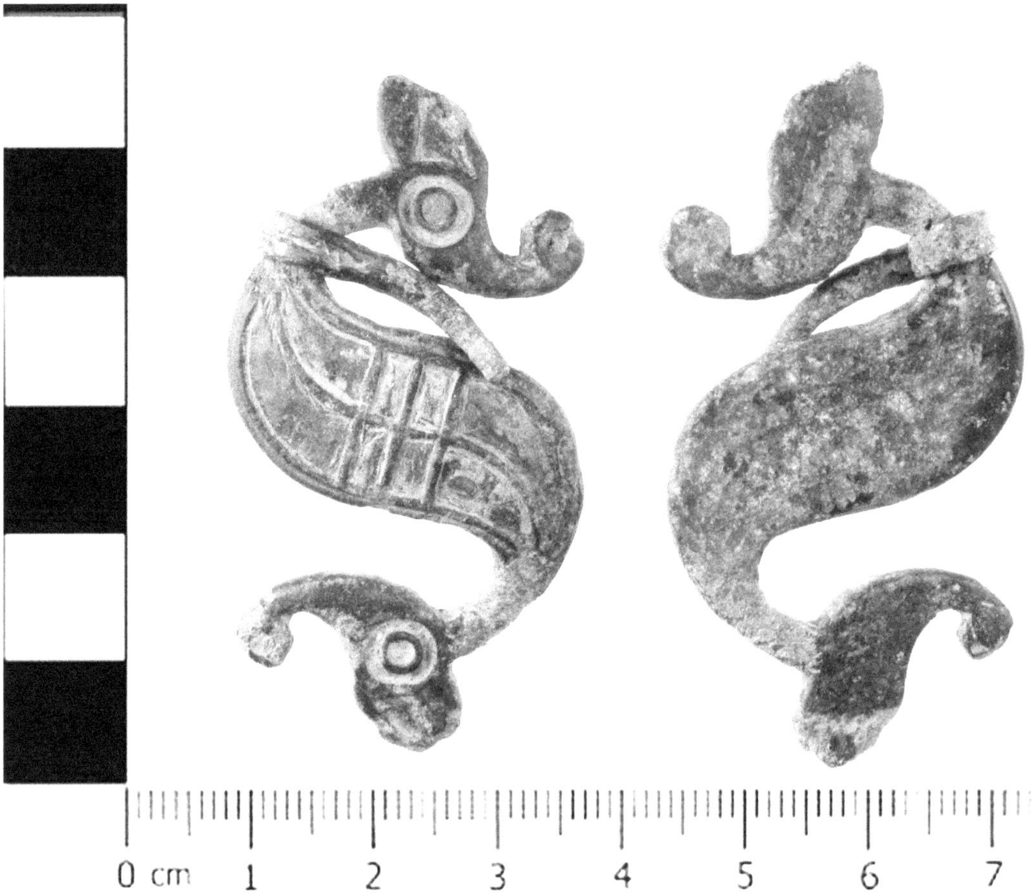

A copper-alloy dragonesque brooch, with enamel decoration. It dates from the period AD 75–175. South Stainley with Cainton, North Yorkshire. PAS: SWYOR-279501. (©Portable Antiquities Scheme [CC BY-Attribution 4.0])

Above left: Copper discs could be highly polished and used to reflect the face of an onlooker. In the Yorkshire Museum (YORYM: 2007.6055). (©York Museums Trust (Yorkshire Museum) [CC BY SA 4.0])

Above right: Metals were melted in large crucibles such as this – it is covered in extra clay to protect it from the high temperatures as well as some of its original contents. In the Yorkshire Museum (YORYM: 2010.393). (©York Museums Trust (Yorkshire Museum))

north of Britain. When they survive, copper alloys are usually degraded on the surface to a green colour. This 'patina' is only a surface discolouration, hiding the original bright, shiny copper beneath. Some of the best evidence for metalworking in York comes from the few surviving crucibles, encrusted with the corroded remains of the molten metals they were used to create. The crucibles are ceramic, but lathered in an extra layer or wall of clay to better protect them from rapid temperature changes. A fantastic group of three, from Toft Green in the *colonia*, were subjected to X-Ray Fluorescence (XRF) in order to identify the materials they contained. The largest contained copper, zinc, tin, and lead, the smallest only copper, tin and zinc; this shows the variations in these metal 'recipes' being used in York. An inscription from nearby Malton records the donation of a goldsmith shop to a slave, presumably by his master when he was freed, showing that even the fanciest goods were made in Yorkshire.

Jet Working

Jet was mentioned in the chapter on magic and religion as a 'magical material'. The quantity of jet objects from Roman York is unrivalled anywhere else in Britain, and some evidence suggests that it was crafted here. Jet naturally outcrops in the North Sea bed. As it is a form of coal, it floats and is moved by tidal pressures towards the East Yorkshire coast, where it can still regularly be found today by beachcombing. If there was an industry attempting to mine the material from the cliffs at Whitby, it was a small-scale cottage industry. Commonly, jet pebbles are no larger than a few centimetres in diameter but larger pieces were available on occasion. The largest fragment of jet known from Roman York is a plank, cut in advance of further working, measuring 90 mm in length. Such a plank would be ideally suited for transportation from the coast towards the major settlement at York to be crafted into rings, bracelets, bangles, pendants, hair pins or miniature statues of animals. It is suspected that the first stage of the journey from the beach to workshop was entirely manual – small pebbles collected and carried in bags or sacks from the beach up the traversable parts of the cliff. It is possible that specialist merchants would bulk-buy the raw materials from a number of individuals before transporting it via road to York.

While jet is difficult to break in the hands, it can easily be carved or ground into shape using metal tools. Circular discs, left over from the production of a bangle or armlets, have a distinctive cutting pattern that shows the use of an iron-tipped lathe in their production. Evidence for lathe cutting, sawing, filing and knife whittling survives on Whitby jet products. It is unclear whether there were ever full-time jet jewellery makers in *Eboracum*. Pragmatism suggests that jewellers and craftsmen working with bone – a material much more commonly available – could turn their hands to jet as a side-line. A suggestion that a jet workshop near the railway station was replaced by a later cemetery on the site is based on the number of unfinished jet products from this area. No single site has been discovered where all the jet was worked as it probably happened in a number of places.

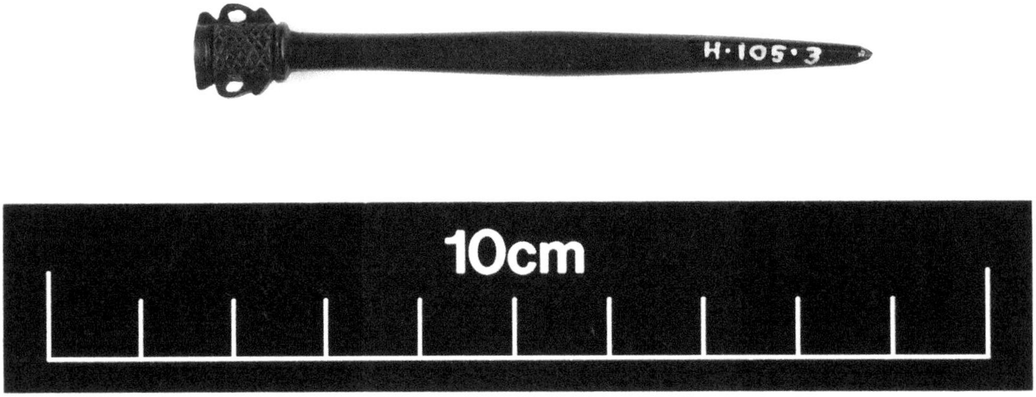

Roman York produced a lot of jet. The head of this example depicts a *cantharus* (a Greek drinking vessel) and it may have been a typically York fashion. Railway station, 1876. In the Yorkshire Museum (YORYM: H105.3). (©York Museums Trust (Yorkshire Museum) [CC BY SA 4.0])

Before it is worked into anything, the raw form of jet looks like small rectangular lumps of coal. These were probably collected from a beach on the Yorkshire coast before being transported to Roman York. Lamb and Lion Hotel, Blossom Street, 1966. In the Yorkshire Museum (YORYM: 1974.116.5). (©York Museums Trust (Yorkshire Museum) [CC BY SA 4.0])

Entertainments

Life in Roman York wasn't all toil and trouble, of course, as ample pursuits existed to help pass the time and provide entertainment for both soldiers and civilians.

Amphitheatre

An amphitheatre is a large, usually oval building, comprising a flat arena surrounded by banked seating. The existence of an amphitheatre at *Eboracum* remains a source of contention among scholars of Roman Britain. There are scant pieces of evidence to suggest that there was one here, but its actual location remains a mystery.

A single piece of literary evidence points to the existence of an amphitheatre in York. A bone plaque inscribed with the Latin inscription DOMINE VICTOR VINCAS FELIX was discovered on the chest of a skeleton buried in a coffin beneath the railway station. A translation of the text reads: 'Master Victor, may you have a lucky win.'

Bone plaque inscribed with a phrase wishing good luck to Victor, from the railway excavations, York. In the Yorkshire Museum (YORYM: H2421). (©York Museums Trust (Yorkshire Museum) [CC BY SA 4.0])

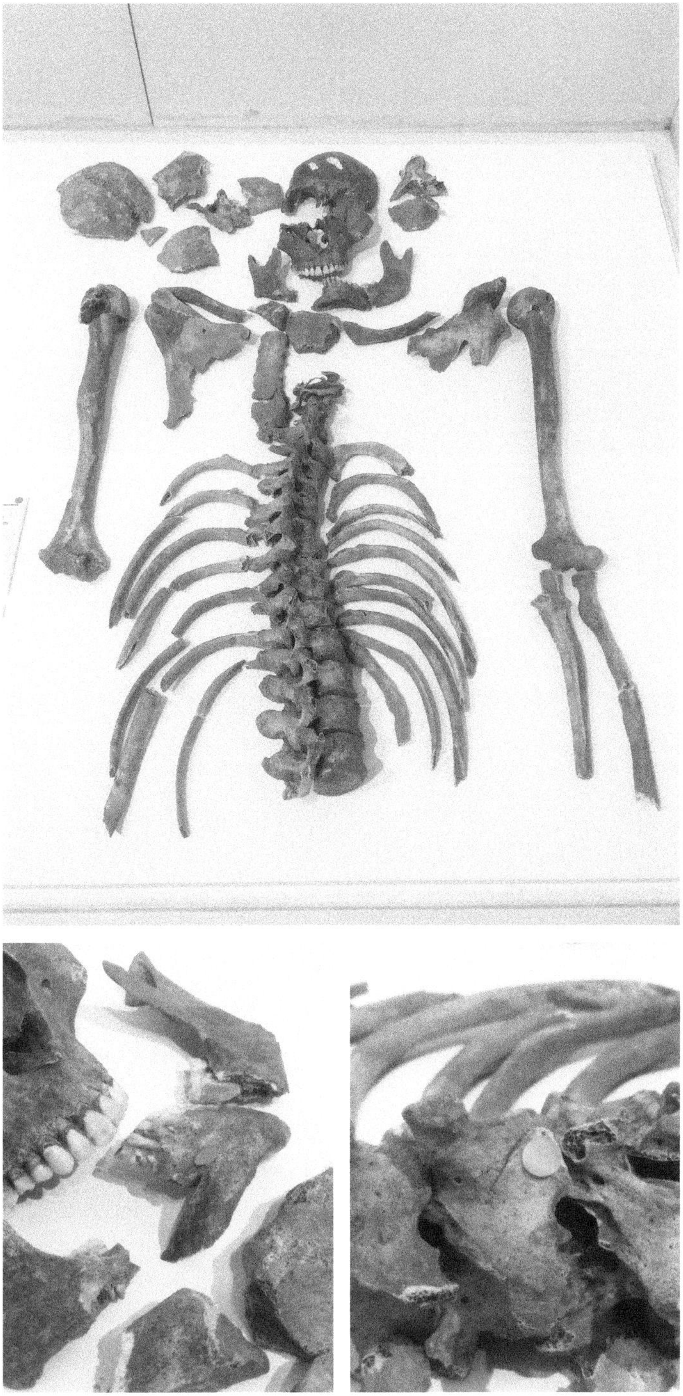

The skeleton of a strongly built man who died a violent death was found underneath the Yorkshire Museum during construction work in 2009. The detail shows the blade marks to his lower jaw and vertebra. In the Yorkshire Museum. (©York Museums Trust (Yorkshire Museum))

This text functioned as a good luck charm, an amulet designed to be pinned onto a showground (or even given to Victor) to help ensure his success, and it is comparable with examples found at the amphitheatre at Caerleon in Wales. Victor may have been a gladiator, fighting in an arena, but may equally have been a boxer, charioteer, wrestler, hunter or sprinter. The donator of the plaque could have been a sporting fan, or had money riding on Victor's success.

Perhaps most revealing is the existence of a the so-called 'Gladiator Cemetery' at Driffield Terrace with its decapitated skeletons and the bite-mark of a large carnivore on the pelvis of one individual – both could be linked with gladiatorial games. Renovations during a major redevelopment of the Yorkshire Museum in 2009–10 unearthed another possible gladiator.

Excavation work below the current basement floor level (the Roman layers in York are quite deep under the modern ground level) revealed the partially preserved remains of a human skeleton. His legs and hands had been removed by a Victorian drain, truncating the surviving remains. His skeleton showed that he was a well-built, physically fit individual who had spent much of his adult life lifting heavy loads. Most interestingly, a series of un-healed wounds on the skeleton showed that he had died a particularly violent death! Cut marks on his spine, vertebra and head show attacks from in front and behind by someone wielding a sharp, bladed weapon – most likely a short sword. His lower right jaw had been ripped away by one attack and he was finished off by a penetrating cut into the skull from behind. The nature of the wounds clearly indicates a violent death by a skilled attacker, though the location in which we find this body is unusual. The Yorkshire Museum resides immediately to the west of the south-west tower of the fortress (the still standing Multangular Tower), and this skeleton had probably been deposited in or next to the huge ditch which surrounded the wall.

So was there an amphitheatre at *Eboracum*? In 1924 Home suggested that a curve preserved in the street layout at Bishophill/Trinity Lane (in the civilian settlement) was due to the presence of an amphitheatre beneath. Wenham, the prolific excavator of York in the 1970s and 80s, argued for the amphitheatre at the west side of the fortress, beneath modern-day Marygate and partially within the museum gardens. The nature and locations of investigations into Roman York have been such that it remains entirely possible that a substantial monumental structure, with a diameter of well over 40 metres could still be hidden beneath York and remain undetected. At this moment in time, we simply do not know.

Reading for Pleasure

We know there was literacy among the inhabitants of Roman York – the tombstones are good evidence of that. What we don't know is how literate most people were; we know that soldiers needed to understand basic record keeping and that the upper classes were probably well educated. The written and spoken word were important forms of entertainment throughout the Roman world; the innumerable plays and poems available to Classicists are testament to that. From York the evidence is scant, but an altar to Silvanus included lines of poetry underneath a dedication to the god.

Bathhouses and Gaming

To the modern reader, the idea of using a bathing complex as a form of recreation seems somewhat alien. Familiar as we are with the idea of group saunas or steam rooms, these are usually related explicitly to pampering, relaxation or sport. The Romano-British bathhouse was a thriving, community experience. Bathing was a protracted process, incorporating a progression between cold rooms to warm rooms, a hot room, a steam room and hot and cold plunge pools to both open and close the pores. Soap was not yet used, but olive oil served as a cleanser. Two bathhouses are known from York: the military bathhouse at the eastern edge of the fortress, partly visible now beneath the Roman Bath pub, and the civilian bathhouse located immediately south of the river.

Male and female bathers did so separately, either at different times of the day or using two different entrances to separate (but functionally identical) buildings. The bathhouse at Leicester, built into the Jewry Wall Museum, operated such a system.

The excavation of a bathhouse drain beneath Church Street in 1972 revealed a great deal about the bathing experience of *Eboracum*. The drain was filled with various pieces of flotsam from the military bathhouse. Broken pottery, from drinking beakers,

A pub built over a Roman bathhouse. (©Carole Raddato via Wikimedia Commons [CC BY-Attribution SA 2.0])

The *caldarium* (hot plunge pool) of the military bathhouse at York. (©Carole Raddato via Wikimedia Commons [CC BY-Attribution SA 2.0])

Intaglios (ring settings) found in the sewer beneath the bathhouse; they have fallen out of finger rings worn by bathing soldiers (not to scale). Church Street, 1972. In the Yorkshire Museum (YORYM: H2225). (©York Museums Trust (Yorkshire Museum) [CC BY SA 4.0])

was prevalent. Changing rooms were communal places and no lockers yet existed by which to securely store clothing – many individuals chose to wear objects of high value throughout the bath in order to better protect them. Evidently this was not wholly successful as many intaglios (ring settings) were located in the Church Street drain, having fallen from the rings of their owner. Intaglios are carved semi-precious jewels, often in red jasper, chalcedony or haematite depicting divine or heroic scenes upon them. The Church Street sewer was also an excellent cache for gaming pieces; over thirty-five circular counters carved from animal bone or broken pottery were recovered. A game similar to draughts/checkers known variously as *ludus latrunculorum*, *latrones*, or *latrunculi* is common in the Roman world and was, evidently, played while bathing.

Bars

Given the tonnage of ceramic fragments excavated from this site, it would be inconceivable to think that a good proportion of them were not used for the purposes of transporting or physically drinking alcohol. Both wine and native beer would have been available and consumed in domestic settings and public establishments. The development of large pedestal beakers, many indented, in the late second century creates a very clear identifier for the rise of beer-drinking in Britain.

The large number of pedestal beakers found in Roman Britain might indicate the rise of beer consumption instead of wine. Railway station, 1872. In the Yorkshire Museum (YORYM: H2225). (©York Museums Trust (Yorkshire Museum) [CC BY SA 4.0])

Brothels

Prostitution is a somewhat invisible industry in Roman York. We assume that it happened but, unfortunately, have no concrete proof where and when it was going on. Wall paintings in Pompeii list the differing prices, in sesterces, of a sexual encounter with a number of ladies in a brothel, many of whom would be slaves or ex-slaves and owned by the brothel-owner. Equally, ancient sources suggest that we should not just think of these spaces as somewhere that men went for sex with women – this idea is incredibly outdated in modern scholarship; we should consider single-sex relations taking place as well as group activities.

If the person selling themselves for sex was a freeborn citizen seeking an interesting profession, they were reduced to the status of *infames* (think 'infamous') and deprived of many legal protections. The existence of phallic wall carvings is often misconstrued as indicators of a house of ill-repute; the evidence from Britain very much points to these being used as a good-luck symbol rather than their use as a shop-sign. Three phallic carvings were excavated from the west side of the fortress wall in York, but these indicate an image protecting the fortress wall itself rather than euphemistically pointing towards the nearest brothel.

Pets

There is a presumption that people kept animals in Roman York but these are very, very difficult to trace archaeologically. For example, there is a small amount of

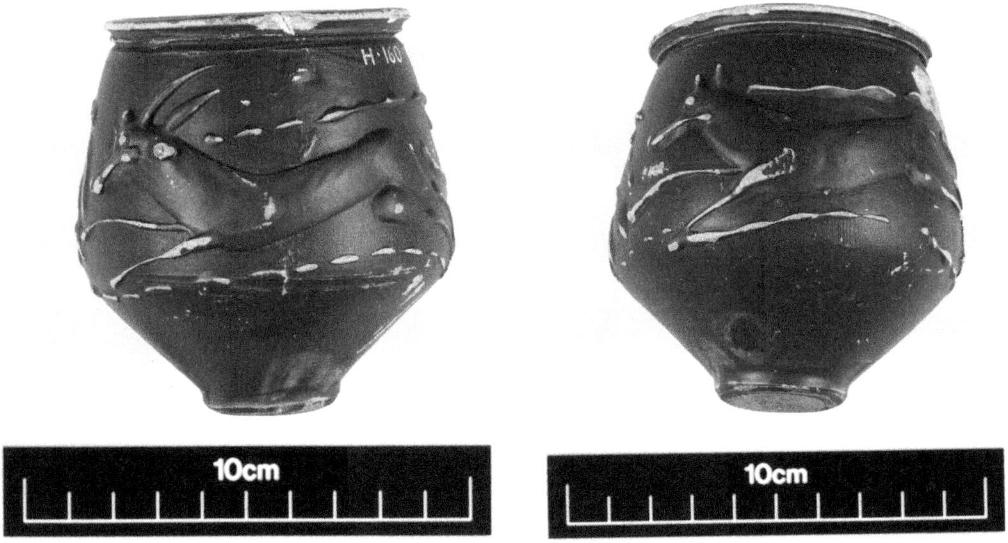

Produced in the Nene Valley in the second to fourth century AD, this sort of beaker depicts a hunting scene – a deer is chased by a hunting hound. Railway station, 1872. In the Yorkshire Museum (YORYM: H160). (©York Museums Trust (Yorkshire Museum) [CC BY SA 4.0])

evidence for horse bones being gnawed by dogs in the early third century, but whether these dogs were pets in the modern sense, feral or somewhere between we can't know. We do know from classical sources and archaeological evidence elsewhere that greyhounds, ferrets, nightingales and parrots were all kept as pets. The writer Strabo wrote that Britain was famous for breeding hunting dogs. Cats too were valued for their pest-control abilities.

Emperors and York

The history of Roman York is quite intimately tied up with the lives of several Roman Emperors. During their brief stays in York, this northern provincial town temporarily became the centre of the entire Roman Empire.

Septimius Severus

(Lived AD 145–211, reigned AD 193–211)

The famous 'Severan tondo', a family portrait depicting the Imperial family – Septimius, Julia, Geta (face removed) and Caracalla. (©Jose Luiz Bernardes Riberio via Wikimedia Commons [CC BY SA 4.0])

Severus came to power in AD 193, having seized control from Pertinax in the Year of the Five Emperors. He is well known for having undertaken a military campaign in Scotland between the years AD 208 and 211, using *Eboracum* as his headquarters. In the early third century York was the largest military installation in the north of Britain and best equipped to deal with the incumbent Imperial family and entourage. Severus brought his wife, Julia Domna, and sons Geta and Caracalla to Britain with him. The campaign

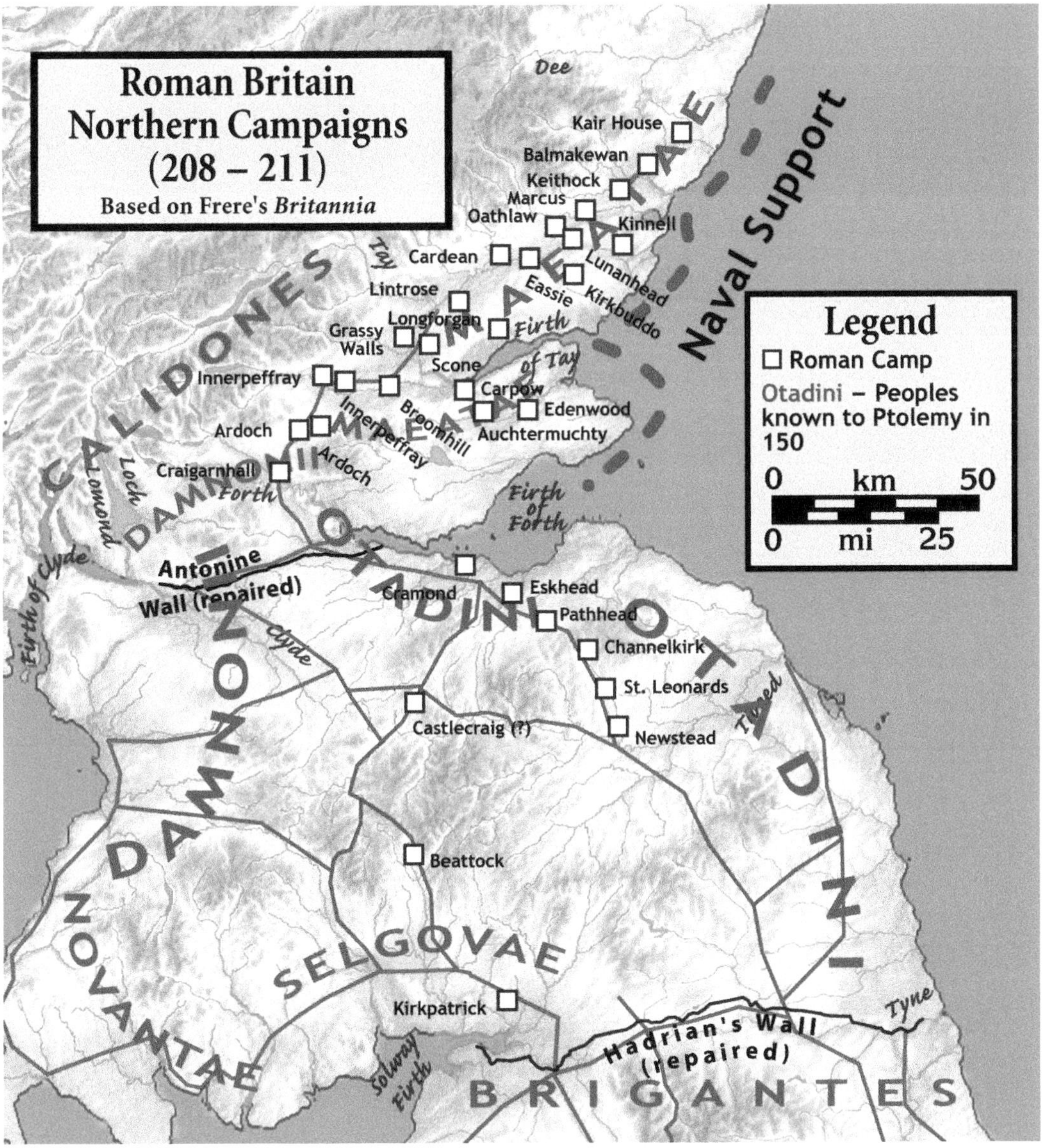

A map showing the Severan military campaign in Scotland. (©Wikimedia Commons [CC BY-SA 3.0])

in Scotland was the largest military force yet brought against the inhabitants north of the Forth–Clyde isthmus and featured the Praetorian Guard (the crack legionary troops usually based in Rome), all of whom returned to York for each winter season. This military campaign was slow, piecemeal and largely overshadowed by the declining health and eventual death of the Emperor in February of 211.

Irrespective of the campaign, for three years in the early third century, York was at the centre of the Roman Empire and the Imperial bureaucracy. The impact the Imperial family had on the archaeological record is significant, to the extent that contemporary reliefs show that the Empress's hairstyle, clothes and manners were copied by the women of Roman Britain. The Severans were from North Africa and were supporters of many eastern gods. The dedication of a new temple to Serapis by Claudius Hieronymianus, *Legatus* of the 6th Legion (and presumably well-known to Severus) is dated from this period. Two unusual head pots have also been associated with the Imperial family, one supposedly depicting Julia Domna with her characteristic parted hairstyle and the other her son (and later Emperor) Caracalla identified by his small chin, pursed lips and diadem.

The death of Septimius Severus in York in AD 211 brought the Imperial link to the city to an abrupt halt. The Roman biographer Cassius Dio quotes the dying Emperor's advice to his two sons: 'Agree with each other, make the soldiers rich, and

An inscription recording the construction of a temple to the god Serapis by Claudius Hieronymianus. In the Yorkshire Museum (YORYM: 1998.27). (©York Museums Trust (Yorkshire Museum) [CC BY SA 4.0])

Figurine of Serapis, depicted as a bearded god wearing a *modius* (grain measure). In the Museo archaeologico nazionale (Florence, Italy). (©Sailko via Wikimedia Commons [CC BY-SA 3.0])

ignore everyone else.' The Emperor was cremated in *Eboracum*, the proceedings of which are again recorded by Dio:

> His body, arrayed in military garb was placed upon a pyre, and as a mark of honour the soldiers and his sons ran about it and as for the soldiers' gifts, those who had things at hand to offer put them upon it and his sons applied the flame.

A hill to the west of the city, where a cremation might be expected to take place, continues to be named 'Severus Hill' and is associated by antiquarian scholars with the site of the cremation, though no modern archaeological investigation has been able to confirm this.

Constantine the Great

(Lived AD 272–337, reigned AD 306–337)
When Constantine first arrived in York, he was not Emperor; much like Geta and Caracalla a century before him, he was travelling as part of the retinue of his father, Emperor Constantius I, but some historical background is required before this can usefully be discussed.

A 1998 statue by sculptor Phillip Jackson, depicting the seated Constantine bearing a sword with a broken tip. On public display outside of York Minster. (©Son of Groucho via Wikimedia Commons [CC BY-attribution 2.0])

In AD 285 the Emperor Diocletian was co-Emperor with Maximian. Many previous Emperors, Severus included, had reigned with co-Emperors as a mechanism to ensure the correct imperial training could be given to a successor, but they were equally in control of the whole Empire. Change came in AD 293 when each Emperor, now known by the title of Augustus, appointed a junior emperor in each of their regions, the Caesar, with whom they halved their individual regions. So in 293 the 'Tetrarchy' came about and the Empire was divided into four sections with the Caesars having the right of succession over their respective Augustus. Maximian's Caesar in charge of Britain and the Gallic provinces was Constantius Chlorus (aka Constantine I, the father of the eventual Constantine the Great).

Constantius was eventually elevated to the rank of Augustus in 305 following the retirement of Maximian, with Flavius Valerius Severus appointed as his Caesar in the Western provinces. He arrived in Britain for the second time in late 305 or early 306 (having previously fought here against the usurper Allectus a decade earlier) and, following a brief military campaign in 305 against the Picts beyond the Antonine Wall, Constantius returned to York for the winter. Unexpectedly, he died in the summer of 306, but before he did he recommended his son Constantine to his legions as his worthy successor. The legions hailed Constantine as Emperor in York immediately, as chronicled by the writer Eutropius. While the senior and junior officers probably pledged their support to Constantine in person within the *principia*, if the whole legion

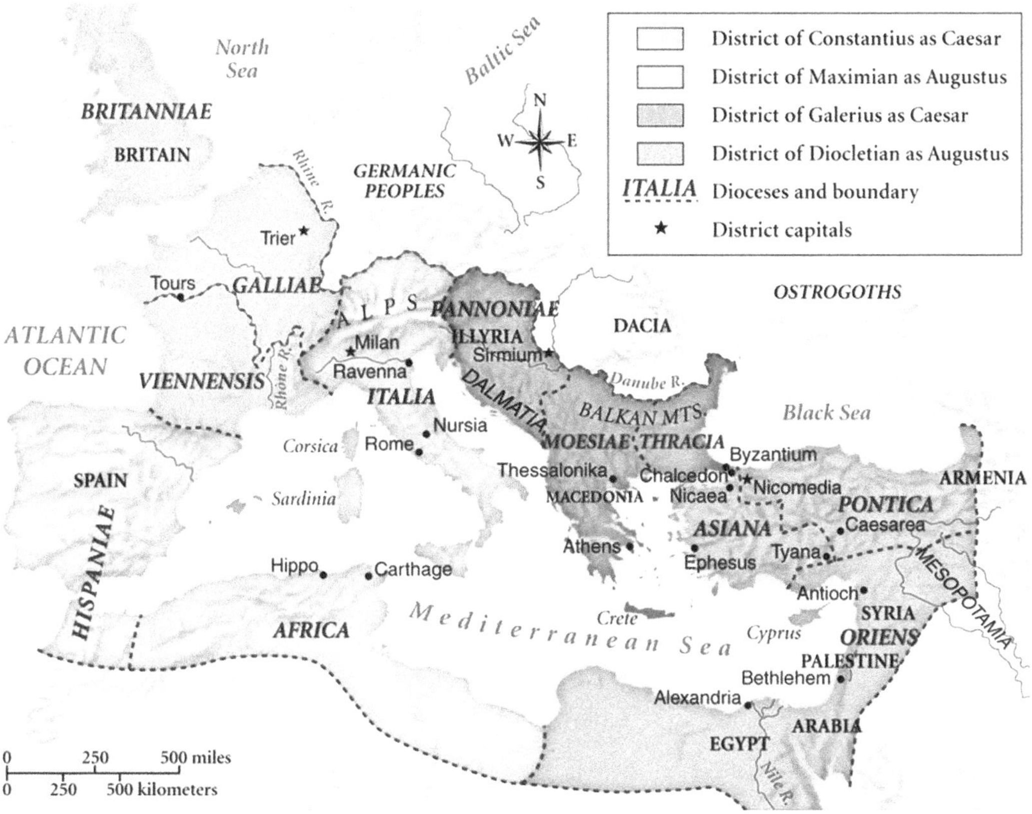

Division of the Roman Empire under the first Tetrarchy, AD 293. Note the western provinces of Constantius Chlorus. (©Coppermine Photo Gallery via Wikimedia Commons [CC BY-Attribution SA 3.0])

had later hailed him as Emperor this probably would have taken place on a parade ground in the immediate vicinity of the fortress somewhere (a firm location has never been pinned down, but any area of reasonably clear, flat land would have sufficed). The proclamation of a Roman Emperor in York is a unique and defining point of York's history and is rightly commemorated by a (now famous) statue of Constantine outside the Minster.

Constantine's accession sparked civil war once again. Constantine was, effectively, a usurper to the Imperial purple toga because the junior emperor to his father was supposed to be made Emperor and Constantine jumped the queue. His actions between 306 and 324 are the source of much intrigue. He eventually managed to facilitate the reconstruction of a single Empire of which he was the sole Emperor. His most notable actions though are the building of an imperial residence at Byzantium and the subsequent renaming of the city as Constantinople (the seat of power for the later Byzantine Empire), the reorganisation of the army and military campaigns against the Franks, Alamanii, Goths and Sarmatians. Most famous of all is the Edict of Milan in 313 which decreed tolerance of the Christian religion – a landmark in the history of Christianity.

Despite his cultural legacy left in York, there is little evidence of major construction in the fortress during the early fourth century, with the exception of the reconfiguration of the *principia*. Constantius and Constantine, not having had access to a purpose-built Imperial Palace, would probably have used the *Praetorium* which housed Severus and the Imperial family a century before.

By the time of Constantine, the Empire had long since stopped expanding and the army had adopted a defence-in-depth approach geared primarily to repelling invaders and making the frontiers secure. The (probably recently installed) *Dux Britanniarum* was probably in charge of all the troops in the north of Britain.

The fourth century also held changes in artistic style, for example, with the development of huge and monumental statues of ruling emperors – a tradition embraced beautifully by Constantine during his long tenure as Emperor. A marble statue head discovered in Stonegate, York (situated beneath the *Via Praetoria*), is thought to depict Constantine the Great. The head is twice life size and would have originally capped a huge statue of Constantine somewhere in the vicinity of the *Praetorium* of the fortress. He is clean shaven and, although now weathered, can still be seen to sport close-cropped hair and a wreath of single oak-leaves. This depiction might be one of the earliest, if not the earliest, depiction of Constantine as Emperor. We know that this statue depicts Constantine the Great through comparison to other statues and depictions of his image on coins. He used the crown of oak leaves, as do his successors, in contrast to earlier Emperors who wore diadems or laurel-wreaths and he is notable as the first Emperor since Trajan (d. AD 117) who did not wear a beard.

Head of a marble statue depicting the Emperor Constantine, from Stonegate, York. In the Yorkshire Museum (YORYM: 1998.23). (©York Museums Trust (Yorkshire Museum) [CC BY SA 4.0])

Appendix

The standing remains of Roman York cannot rival those of Hadrian's Wall or of sites which were abandoned and never much built upon, like Calleva or Caerleon. Much of the structural wealth of *Eboracum* remains hidden and protected beneath the early medieval and medieval layers of the city's history. That being said, two centuries of investigation have not left us without interesting Roman archaeological remains to engage with.

York Minster

The Minster building dominates the skyline of the city and is located centrally, and many of the modern streets provide direct access to it. Both features owe a debt to the position of the Roman *principia* building, atop which it directly sits. The Undercroft of the Minster offers a small selection of the Roman remains excavated from the site between 1966 and 1973, presented in a sympathetic and engaging manner. Fragments of the *basilica* building have been consolidated and are dotted throughout the gallery (which is, admittedly, focussed on the medieval period). A column from the building is re-erected outside of the Minster, opposite the modern statue commemorating Constantine on his throne. Entrance to the museum is included with entry to the Minster.

Yorkshire Museum

Housing the largest collection of Roman material from York, the Yorkshire Museum's Roman galleries focus on the people and material culture of *Eboracum*. Many of the exhibits feature objects discovered during antiquarian excavations, particularly related to the various cemetery sites. Star objects on permanent display include the marble statue head of Constantine the Great, the tombstone of Lucius Duccius Rufinus and the Four Seasons mosaic. The museum offers a regular series of talks for adults, and family activities during school holidays. The museum charges for entry, but up to three children go free with each adult.

Museum Gardens

The Victorian botanical gardens in which the Yorkshire Museum is situated is the location of the Multangular Tower, clearly visible and accessible and a must for any explorer investigating Roman York. The gardens also include a number of plain sarcophagi of Roman date dotted throughout, though these are used primarily as decorative elements in the garden rather than formal museum displays. The walls next to the city library, behind the Multangular Tower, can also be accessed from here. The gardens are free and accessible to all, but close at dusk.

Roman Bath

Remains of the legionary bathhouse are situated underneath the aptly named Roman Bath pub, off St Sampson's Square in the centre of York. It is a small, independent museum but houses some of the best preserved Roman architecture in York.

City Walls

Walking the city walls is the best way to get a sense of scale for the Roman town as they follow the Roman fortress and *colonia* walls in part and are well signposted, well visited and well looked after. There are several points in the city to gain access to or from the walls, though the northern section from Bootham Bar to Mickelgate Bar and then onto Jewbury/Foss Islands Road is particularly recommended. A small section of the western gatehouse is visible under a glass floor in the café at Bootham Bar. The walls are free to access, but are not wheelchair or pushchair friendly, and are locked at dusk.

Recommended Resources

All of the collections of the Yorkshire Museum are released online. Images are downloadable under a Creative Commons by Share Alike licence and are thus free to use. http://www.yorkmuseumstrust.org.uk/collections/

The Portable Antiquities Scheme is a nationally funded organisation which aims to record and publish online archaeological objects found by members of the public. Often, this means objects found by metal detector. There are over a million objects recorded online from across England, including nearly a quarter of a million Roman objects. Free to use, it is the single largest open-access archaeological catalogue available to archaeologists. http://finds.org.uk

Select Introductory Bibliography

Allason-Jones, L. *Roman Jet in the Yorkshire Museum*
de la Bédoyère, G. 2002. *Gods and Thunderbolts*
Bishop, M. C. 2014. *The Secret History of the Roman Roads of Britain*
Hoffmann, B. 2013. *The Invasion of Roman Britain, Archaeology Vs. History*
Mattingly, D. 2006. *Imperial Possession*
Ottaway, P. 2012. *Roman York*
Ottaway, P. 2014. *Roman Yorkshire*
Toynbee, J. M. C. 1971. *Death and Burial in the Roman World*

About the Author

Adam Parker is the Assistant Curator of Archaeology at the Yorkshire Museum, where he has worked since 2010. He is currently well over a decade into his relationship with Roman archaeology – a journey which started at Durham 6th Form Centre, then travelled through the University of Leicester for four years to study BA (Hons) Ancient History and Archaeology and MA Rome & Its Neighbours before reaching York. In a professional capacity he works with archaeological collections from York and North Yorkshire and regularly teaches and gives talks on prehistoric, Roman, and both early and later medieval archaeology to adults of all ages. His academic studies are in the material culture of Roman magic in Britain and the north-west provinces of the Roman Empire, which is the topic of his current PhD studies with the Open University.